ORACLE® DBA SQL

QUICK REFERENCE

Prentice Hall

ORACLE DBA SQL QUICK REFERENCE SERIES

Oracle DBA SQL Quick Reference
Russel ▪ Cordingley

Oracle DBA Backup and Recovery
Quick Reference
Russel ▪ Cordingley

Oracle DBA Scripting
Quick Reference
Russel ▪ Cordingley

ORACLE DBA SQL
QUICK REFERENCE

RUSSEL ■ CORDINGLEY

PRENTICE
HALL
PTR

Prentice Hall

Professional Technical Reference

Upper Saddle River NJ 07458

www.phptr.com

Library of Congress Cataloging-in-Publication Data is available.

A CIP catalog record for this book can be obtained from the Library of Congress.

Editorial/Production Supervision: *Patti Guerrieri*
Interior Design: *Gail Cocker-Bogusz*
Cover Design Director: *Jerry Votta*
Cover Design: *Nina Scuderi*

Acquisitions Editor: *Jeffrey Pepper*
Editorial Assistant: *Linda Ramagnano*
Manufacturing Manager: *Alexis R. Heydt-Long*
Marketing Manager: *Dan DePasquale*

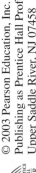

© 2003 Pearson Education, Inc.
Publishing as Prentice Hall Professional Technical Reference
Upper Saddle River, NJ 07458

Prentice Hall PTR offers excellent discounts on this book when ordered in quantity for bulk purchases or special sales. For more information, please contact: U.S. Corporate and Government Sales, 1-800-382-3419, corpsales@pearsontechgroup.com. For sales outside of the U.S., please contact: International Sales, 1-317-581-3793, international@pearsontechgroup.com.

Printed in the United States of America

First Printing

ISBN 0-13-140303-6

Pearson Education Ltd.
Pearson Education Australia Pty. Limited
Pearson Education Singapore, Pte. Ltd.
Pearson Education North Asia Ltd.

Pearson Education Canada, Ltd.
Pearson Educación de Mexico, S.A. de C.V.
Pearson Education — Japan
Pearson Education Malaysia, Pte. Ltd.

Charlie would like to dedicate this book to Ed Holbrook whose vision and support allowed me to be what I am today. Thank you, Ed. You make the world a better place for your being in it.

Contents

Chapter Two
SQL Command Reference

Introduction

The Oracle database and the Structured Query Language (SQL) that it supports are complex and ever changing products that have grown increasingly complex and powerful over the years. This book is not an attempt to teach the new Database Administrator (DBA) everything she or he needs to know about how to administer an Oracle database. That would be an interesting book challenge, but not the one we wanted to tackle. Instead, we wrote the book we've both been wishing we had, but couldn't find anywhere. A simple reference to the Oracle version of SQL and some of the critical tables and views that the practicing Oracle DBA needs every day. This is a purely syntax reference, a quick way to get a reminder of what options a command takes and the exact syntax required.

Most Oracle DBAs spend probably 90% of their time doing less than 5% of the tasks possible with an Oracle database. They neither need nor want a book to give them the syntax for those commands they use every day. But for the commands they may only use once every six months or so, a little quick reminder can be helpful. And that's the purpose and intent of this book—to give the working DBA a *little* book that they can keep on their desktop or next to the server where they can quickly look up the syntax for the command they need, or find the right name for the view they know exists, but haven't had to use since the last time there was a problem.

As Oracle has grown from our first days with Oracle 6 to the complexity and power of Oracle 9*i*, the number of new commands, and options and modifiers to the old ones, has grown enormously. If you're like us, you know there are new options and ways to do things, but often need a quick reminder of the syntax or options available. We hope you'll find this book a useful tool for that.

HOW TO USE THIS BOOK

This book is divided up into three basic sections:

- Chapter 1—covers the operators and functions recognized by Oracle SQL, as well as the format models, privileges and reserved words, organized into easy to read tables and grouped by the type of function, operator, privilege, or format model involved.

- Chapter 2—is a complete SQL command reference, showing the syntax and options for every Oracle SQL command supported by Oracle 9.2 from ALTER CLUSTER to UPDATE, in alphabetical order. We have used standard "railroad" syntax diagrams to make it easy to follow the options and syntax required.

- Chapter 3—is a listing of the data dictionary views that are a part of every DBA's life, and the dynamic performance tables that provide a wealth of information about what is happening inside the database. In the interest of keeping to our design goal of making this a short, easy-to-use and quick reference, we stuck to a simple listing of the tables and views here. The names make it pretty clear what each covers, and as working DBAs we've found that's really all we need. Once we know the name, a simple DESCRIBE will get the rest.

A note on the syntax diagrams in Chapter 2. Certain clauses show up across a wide range of commands with no change in the syntax or options they support. In order to keep the diagrams as simple as possible, we have grouped those clauses at the end of the chapter under "Common." The clauses covered there are:

- Allocate Extent
- Constraints
- Deallocate Unused
- File Specification
- Logging
- Parallel
- Physical Attributes
- Storage

Within each command, we have broken out the syntax for the less common clauses immediately following the main command. This enables a simpler and more readable diagram while providing full information. We have underlined the names of subordinate clauses in the diagrams to make it clear that you need to break out of the main diagram for the syntax to that clause.

TALK TO US

We have made every attempt in this short volume to provide as complete a reference as we could, always with the goal of keeping it quick and easy to find the information you need. Our goal was to give the working Oracle DBA a tool that would make them more productive and we sincerely hope you find it useful. Every effort has been made to be both complete and accurate. If you do find an error or omission or have any comment on the book, we very much want to hear from you. Please write us at: SQLReference@Scribes.com. We don't promise to answer every question or comment, but we do read them and very much appreciate them.

ACKNOWLEDGMENTS

This book is not the work of one or two people, but an entire team, many of whom we, as authors, never get to meet in person, but to whom we are indebted. First we'd like to thank our agent on this book, Neil J. Salkind, of Studio B. It's due to his persistence and advocacy that this book came about.

From Prentice Hall, Jeffrey Pepper, with the assistance of Linda Ramagnano, did an exceptional job taking over a project that had gotten sidetracked. Gail Cocker did the great design in the face of a difficult and different kind of content. And we much appreciate the work of Patti Guerrieri who put it all together.

Over the years we have been honored to work with some truly outstanding Oracle DBAs, especially Quin Bligh, Mahesh Chenga Reddy, Prashant Dangash, and Ross Woody. Each has had a positive impact on this book and beyond. We truly appreciate their professional abilities and their friendship. Our deepest thanks to Maggie Verdier, a wonderful person, a great Oracle DBA, and the technical reviewer for this book.

Chapter One

Programmatic and General Reference

OPERATORS

Oracle supports a number of built in operators that fall into basic categories—simple arithmetic operators, comparison operators, logical operators, and operators that are used in select statements. In Oracle 9, support for User Defined Operators was also added.

Arithmetic Operators

Table 1-1 Arithmetic Operators

Operator	What it does
+ (unary)	Specifies a positive number or expression
− (unary)	Specifies a negative number or expression
+ (binary)	Addition
− (binary)	Subtraction
*	Multiplication
/	Division

Logical Operators

Table 1-2 Logical Operators

Operator	What it does
||	Concatenates two character (string) values
NOT	Reverses the meaning of another logical expression's result
OR	Logical OR—True if any are true, false else
AND	Logical AND—True if all are true, else false

Comparison Operators

Table 1-3 Comparison Operators

Operator	What it does
=	true if two expressions are equal
!= ^= -= <>	logically equivalent—true if two expressions are not equal
>	True if left expression is greater than right expression
>=	True if left expression is greater than or equal to right expression
<	True if left expression is less than right expression
<=	True if left expression is less than or equal to right expression
IN	Is equal to any member of a set or subquery
NOT IN	Does NOT equal any member of a set or subquery
ANY, SOME	True if one or more of the values in the list of expressions or subquery satisfies the condition
ALL	True if all of the values in the list of expressions or subquery satisfies the condition
BETWEEN x AND y	True if greater than or equal to x and less than or equal to y (can be reversed in meaning with NOT)

Table 1-3 Comparison Operators (continued)

Operator	What it does
EXISTS	True if the subquery returns at least one row (can be reversed in meaning with NOT)
LIKE *pattern* [ESCAPE '*c*']	True if expression or subquery matches *pattern*. '%' matches any sequence of characters, '_' matches any single character. If ESCAPE is used, the character '*c*' causes the character following to be taken literally (can be reversed in meaning with NOT).
IS NULL	TRUE if the value is NULL (can be reversed in meaning with NOT)

Select Operators

Also called *SET* operators

Table 1-4 Select Operators (Sets)

Operator	What it does
UNION	This combines the results of two queries and returns the set of distinct rows returned by either query
UNION ALL	This combines the results of two queries and returns all rows returned by either query, including duplicates
INTERSECT	This combines the results of two queries and returns the set of distinct rows returned by both queries
MINUS	This combines the results of two queries and returns the distinct rows that were in the first query, but not in the second

Table 1-5 Other Select Operators

Operator	What it does
(+)	Denotes that the preceding column is an outer join
*	Wildcard operator. Equals all columns in a select statement
PRIOR	Denotes a parent-child relationship in a tree-structured query
ALL	Include all duplicate rows in a query (the default)
DISTINCT	Eliminate duplicates in a result set

Precedence

Oracle evaluates expressions based on the order of precedence. Parentheses () override normal precedence. Lines are evaluated left to right for operators of equal precedence if there are no parentheses to override that order.

SQL Operator Precedence

+ –	Unary arithmetic operators	PRIOR operator
* /	Arithmetic operators	
+ –	Binary arithmetic operators	‖ character operator

All comparison operators

NOT	Logical operator
AND	Logical operator
OR	Logical operator

Arithmetic Operator Precedence

+ –	Unary
* /	
+ –	Binary

FUNCTIONS

Functions, like operators, act on data to return a result. However, unlike operators, functions can operate on zero, one, or more arguments. Of the built in SQL functions in Oracle 9i, there are single row functions, aggregate functions, analytical functions and object reference functions. User defined functions, that can be written in PL/SQL or Java in Oracle 9i, are not covered here.

Single Row Functions

Number Functions

Table 1-6 Single Row Number Functions

Function	What it does
ABS(n)	Returns absolute value of n
ACOS(n)	Returns arc cosine of n in radians
ASIN(n)	Returns arc sine of n in radians
ATAN(n)	Returns arc tangent of n, in radians
ATAN2(n,m)	Returns the arc tangent of n and m, in radians
BITAND(n,m)	Computes the bitwise logical AND of the bits of n and m, where n and m are nonnegative integers. Returns an integer.
CEIL(n)	Ceiling function—returns the smallest integer >= n
COS(n)	Returns the cosine of n where n is in radians
COSH(n)	Returns the hyperbolic cosine of n where n is in radians
EXP(n)	Returns e^n
FLOOR(n)	Returns the largest integer <= n
LN(n)	Returns the natural log of n
LOG(m,n)	Returns the base m log of n
MOD(m,n)	Returns the modulus of m, n—the remainder of m divided by n. (Returns m when $n=0$)
POWER(m,n)	Returns m raised to the nth power
ROUND ($m[,n]$)	Rounds m to the nearest n places. Where n is omitted, default is zero. n must be an integer
SIGN(n)	For $n < 0$, returns -1, for $n > 0$, returns 1, for $n = 0$, returns 0

Table 1-6 Single Row Number Functions (continued)

Function	What it does
SIN(*n*)	Returns sine(*n*) where *n* is in radians
SINH(*n*)	Returns the hyperbolic sine(*n*) where *n* is in radians
SQRT(*n*)	Returns the square root of *n*
TAN(*n*)	Returns the tangent(*n*) where *n* is in radians
TANH(*n*)	Returns the hyperbolic tangent(*n*) where *n* is in radians
TRUNC (*m*[,*n*])	Truncate. Returns *m* truncated to *n* places. Where *n* is omitted, it returns the integer value of *m*.
WIDTH_BUCKET (*exp,min,max,num*)	Returns the "bucket" in which *exp* belongs, where *min* is the minimum value, *max* is the maximum value, and *num* is the number of divisions (buckets) to use

Character Functions

Table 1-7 Character Single Row Functions

Function	What it does
CHR (*n*)	Returns the character whose binary value is *n*. Accepts USING NCHAR_CS clause
CONCAT (*char1,char2*)	Combines two strings, *char1* and *char2*
INITCAP(*char*)	Returns *char* with the first character of each word in *char* capitalized
LOWER(*char*)	Returns *char* with all characters converted to lowercase
LPAD(*char1,n*[,*char2*])	Returns *char1* padded on the left to width *n* with character sequence in *char2*. Default padding is a single blank (space).
LTRIM(*char*[,*set*])	Returns *char* with initial characters in *set* removed from the left. Default *set* is a blank character (space).

Table 1-7   Character Single Row Functions (continued)

Function	What it does
NLS_INITCAP(*char[,nlsparam]*)	Returns *char* with the first character of each word in *char* capitalized. Accepts an NLS parameter.
NLS_LOWER(*char[,nlsparam]*)	Returns *char* with all characters converted to lowercase. Accepts an NLS parameter.
NLSSORT(*char[,nlsparam]*)	Returns language specific sort of *char*. Accepts an NLS parameter.
NLS_UPPER(*char[,nlsparam]*)	Returns *char* with all characters converted to uppercase. Accepts an NLS parameter.
REPLACE(*char[,searchstring[,replacestring]]*)	Returns *char* with *searchstring* replaced by *replacestring*. Where *replacestring* is omitted or null, all instances of *searchstring* are removed. Where *searchstring* is omitted or null, *char* is returned.
RPAD(*char1,n[,char2]*)	Returns *char1* padded on the right to width *n* with character sequence in *char2*. Default padding is a single blank (space).
RTRIM(*char[,set]*)	Returns *char* with initial characters in *set* removed from the right. Default *set* is a blank character (space).
SOUNDEX(*char*)	Returns the phonetic equivalent of *char*. Allows for searches for words that sound alike but are spelled differently.
SUBSTR(*string,n[,m]*) also: SUBSTRB - bytes SUBSTRC - unicode SUBSTR2 - UCS2 codepoints SUBSTR4 - UCS4 codepoints	Returns the substring of *string*, starting at position *n*, for a length of *m* (or to the end of *string* if *m* is not present)
TRANSLATE(*char,from,to*)	Returns *char*, with all occurrences of characters in the *from* string replaced with the corresponding character in the *to* string. If *to* is shorter than *from*, then *from* characters without a corresponding *to* character will be removed. Empty *to* returns NULL, not an empty string.

Table 1-7 Character Single Row Functions (continued)

Function	What it does
TREAT(*exp* AS [[REF] [*schema.*]] *type*)	Changes the declared type of *exp* to *type*
TRIM([[LEADING|TRAILING|BOTH] [*trimchar*] FROM] *source*)	Returns *source* with leading and/or trailing *trimchars* removed. Default *trimchar* is a blank space, default action is to remove both leading and trailing blank spaces.
UPPER (*char*)	Returns *char* with all characters converted to uppercase
ASCII (*char*)	Returns the number value of the first character of *char*
INSTR(*str,substr[,pos[,occur]]*) also: INSTRB - *bytes* INSTRC - *unicode* INSTR2 - *UCS2 codepoints* INSTR4 - *UCS4 codepoints*	"In string" function. Returns the position of the occurrence *occur* of *substr* in *str*, starting at *pos*. Default for *pos* and *occur* is 1. If *pos* is negative, search works backwards from the end of *str*.
LENGTH (*char*) also: LENGTHB - *bytes* LENGTHC - *unicode* LENGTH2 - *UCS2 codepoints* LENGTH4 - *UCS4 codepoints*	Returns the length of *char*

Date Functions

Table 1-8   Date Single Row Functions

Function	What it does
ADD_MONTHS(*d,n*)	Returns the date *d* plus *n* months. If *d* is the last day of the month, or *d+n* would be past the end of the month, returns the last day of the month.
CURRENT_DATE	Returns the current Gregorian date as datatype DATE, in the session specific time zone
CURRENT_TIMESTAMP *[(precision)]*	Returns the current date and time as datatype TIMESTAMP WITH TIME ZONE, in the session specific time zone. *Precision* defaults to 6 places.
DBTIMEZONE	Returns the time zone of the database
EXTRACT (*datetime* FROM *expr*)	*datetime* can be YEAR, MONTH, DAY, HOUR, MINUTE, SECOND, TIMEZONE_HOUR, TIMEZONE_MINUTE, TIMEZONE_REGION, or TIMEZONE_ABBR, and *expr* can be either an internal value or datetime value expression
FROM_TZ(*timestamp, time_zone*)	Returns *timestamp* converted to a TIMESTAMP WITH TIME ZONE value, using *time_zone*
LAST_DAY(*date*)	Returns the date of the last day of the month containing *date*
LOCALTIMESTAMP *[(precision)]*	Returns the current date and time of the session in datatype TIMESTAMP of *precision*
MONTHS_BETWEEN(*date1, date2*)	Returns the number of months between *date1* and *date2*
NEW_TIME(*date,zone1,zone2*)	Returns *date* converted from time zone *zone1* to *zone2*. NLS_DATE_FORMAT must be set to a 24-hour format.
NEXT_DAY(*date,weekday*)	Returns the next *weekday* later than *date* where *weekday* is the day of the week or its abbreviation
NUMTODSINTERVAL (*n, char*)	Returns *n* converted to an INTERVAL DAY TO SECOND literal. *char* can be 'DAY,' 'HOUR,' 'MINUTE,' or 'SECOND,' or an expression that resolves to one of those

Table 1-8 Date Single Row Functions (continued)

Function	What it does
NUMTOYMINTERVAL (*n, char*)	Returns *n* converted to an INTERVAL YEAR TO MONTH literal. *char* can be 'MONTH' or 'YEAR' or an expression that resolves to one of those
ROUND (*date[,fmt]*)	Returns *date* rounded to the nearest unit specified by the format model *fmt*. Defaults to the nearest day.
SESSIONTIMEZONE	Returns the time zone of the current session, either as a time zone offset or a time zone region name, depending on the format used for the most recent ALTER SESSION statement
SYS_EXTRACT_UTC (*datetz*)	Extracts the UTC value of *datetz* where *datetz* is a datetime with time zone displacement
SYSDATE	Returns the current date and time
SYSTIMESTAMP	Returns the system timestamp in TIMESTAMP WITH TIME ZONE datatype
TO_DSINTERVAL(*char [nlsparm]*)	Converts *char* to an INTERVAL DAY TO SECOND type
TO_TIMESTAMP (*char[,fmt[nlsparm]]*)	Converts *char* to datatype of TIMESTAMP. *fmt* specifies the format of *char* if other than the default for datatype TIMESTAMP
TO_TIMESTAMP_TZ (*char[,fmt[nlsparm]]*)	Converts *char* to datatype of TIMESTAMP WITH TIME ZONE. *fmt* specifies the format of *char* if other than the default for datatype TIMESTAMP WITH TIME ZONE.
TO_YMINTERVA(*char*)	Converts *char* to an INTERVAL YEAR TO MONTH type
TRUNC (*date[,fmt]*)	Returns *date* truncated to the time unit specified by *fmt*. If *fmt* is omitted, *date* is truncated to the nearest day.
TZ_OFFSET(*tzname | SESSIONTIMEZONE | DBTIMEZONE | '+|-hh:mi'*)	Returns the timezone offset

Conversion Functions

Table 1-9 Conversion Single Row Functions

Function	What it does
ASCIISTR(*string*)	Returns the ASCII string in the database language of *string* which can be in any character set. Non-ASCII characters are converted to their UTF-16 binary values.
BIN_TO_NUM(*expr[,expr...]*)	Converts the binary bits of *expr,expr...* to a number. Example: BIN_TO_NUM(1,1,0,1) returns 13.
CAST(*expr	MULTISET] (subquery) AS type*)	Converts from one built in datatype or collection type to another
CHARTOROWID(*char*)	Converts *char* to type ROWID
COMPOSE('*string*')	Converts *string* to its Unicode string equivalent in the same character set
CONVERT(*char, dest_set [,source_set]*)	Returns *char* converted from *source_set* character set to *dest_set* character set. If *source_set* is not specified, the database character set is assumed.
DECOMPOSE(*string [CANONICAL | COMPATIBILITY]*)	Returns a unicode *string* decomposed from its fully normalized form. If CANONICAL(the default) is used, the result can be recomposed with COMPOSE.
HEXTORAW (*char*)	Returns hexadecimal digits of *char* as RAW
NUMTODSINTERVAL (*n, char*)	Converts number *n* to an INTERVAL DAY TO SECOND literal. *char* can be 'DAY,' 'HOUR,' 'MINUTE,' or 'SECOND'
NUMTOYMINTERVAL (*n, char*)	Converts number *n* to an INTERVAL YEAR TO MONTH *literal. char* can be 'YEAR or 'MONTH'
RAWTOHEX(*raw*)	Converts *raw* to its hexadecimal equivalent character value
RAWTONHEX(*raw*)	Converts *raw* to its hexadecimal equivalent NVARCHAR2 character value
ROWIDTOCHAR(*rowid*)	Converts *rowid* to a VARCHAR2 18 characters long
ROWIDTONCHAR(*rowid*)	Converts *rowid* to a NVARCHAR2 18 characters long

Table 1-9   Conversion Single Row Functions (continued)

Function	What it does
TO_CHAR (nchar | clob | nclob)	Converts an NCHAR, NVARCHAR2, CLOB or NCLOB value to the underlying database character set
TO_CHAR (date [,fmt[nlsparm]])	Converts *date* to VARCHAR2, using format *fmt* and any *nlsparm*
TO_CHAR (num [,fmt[nlsparm]])	Converts *num* to VARCHAR2, using format *fmt* and any *nlsparm*
TO_CLOB (lob_col|char)	Converts lob_col or char to CLOB value
TO_DATE char [,fmt[nlsparm]]	Converts *char* to a date, using the format *fmt* and any *nlsparm*. If *fmt* is not specified, then the default date format is used.
TO_DSINTERVAL (char [nlsparm])	Converts *char* to an INTERVAL DAY TO SECOND literal
TO_LOB(long_col)	Converts the LONG or LONG RAW value of *long_col* to LOB values
TO_MULTI_BYTE(char)	Converts single byte *char* to multibyte characters
TO_NCHAR(char [,fmt[nlsparm]])	Converts a string from the database character set to the national character set
TO_NCHAR (datetime | interval[,fmt[nlsparm]])	Converts a date, time, or interval value from the database character set to the national character set
TO_NCHAR (n [,fmt[nlsparm]])	Converts a number to a string in the NVARCHAR2 character set
TO_NCLOB (lob_column | char)	Converts *char* or *lob_column* to NCLOB data, using the national character set
TO_NUMBER(char[,fmt[nlsparm]])	Converts *char* to a number, using *fmt* as the format specifier
TO_SINGLE_BYTE(char)	Returns *char* with any multibyte characters converted to the corresponding single byte characters

Table 1-9 Conversion Single Row Functions (continued)

Function	What it does
TO_YMINTERVAL(char [nlsparm])	Converts char to an INTERVAL YEAR TO MONTH literal
TRANSLATE (text USING CHAR_CS | NCHAR_CS)	Returns text translated into the database character set (USING CHAR_CS) or the national character set (USING NCHAR_CS)
UNISTR(string)	Returns string in Unicode using the database Unicode character set

Miscellaneous Single Row Functions

Table 1-10 Miscellaneous Single Row Functions

Function	What it does
BFILENAME('dir','fname')	Returns a locator for an LOB binary file on the filesystem. dir is the database object that is an alias for the full pathname of the file directory. fname is the actual file name.
COALESCE(expr[,expr,...])	Returns the first nonnull expression in a list of expressions
DECODE(expr,search,result [,search,result...][,default])	Searches expr for search, returning the specific result for each search. Returns default if search is not found.
DEPTH(correlation_int)	Returns the number of levels in the path specified by an UNDER_PATH condition
DUMP(expr[,return_fmt [,start[,length]]])	Returns a VARCHAR2 value with the datatype, length, and internal representation of expr, using the format of return_fmt. Returns entire internal representation unless start and optionally length are specified.
EMPTY_BLOB()	Returns a locator for a BLOB, allowing you to initialize the BLOB
EMPTY_CLOB()	Returns a locator for a CLOB, allowing you to initialize the CLOB

Table 1-10   Miscellaneous Single Row Functions (continued)

Function	What it does
EXISTSNODE(*XML_Instance, path [expr]*)	Walks the XML tree and returns success if a node is found that matches the specified *path*
EXTRACT (*XML_Instance, path [expr]*)	Walks the XML tree and, if nodes are found which match the specified *path*, returns those nodes
EXTRACTVALUE(*XML_Instance, path [expr]*)	Walks the XML tree and, if nodes are found that match the specified *path*, returns the scalar value of those nodes
GREATEST(*expr1,expr,...]*)	Returns the expression in the list with greatest value. All data types are implicitly converted to the data type of the first expression. Character comparisons use the database character set.
LEAST(*expr1,expr...]*)	Returns the expression in the list with least value. All data types are implicitly converted to the data type of the first expression. Character comparisons use the database character set.
NLS_CHARSET_DECL_LEN (*bytes,set_id*)	Returns the declaration width of the NCHAR column of width *bytes* and a character set ID of *set_id*
NLS_CHARSET_ID(*text*)	Returns the number of a character set ID with a character set name of *text*
NLS_CHARSET_NAME(*num*)	Returns the character set name of the character set with ID *num*
NULLIF(*expr1,expr2*)	Returns null if *expr1* and *expr2* are equal, else returns *expr1*
NVL(*expr1,expr2*)	Returns *expr2* if *expr1* is NULL, else returns *expr1*
NVL2(*expr1,expr2,expr3*)	Returns *expr2* if *expr1* is NOT NULL, else returns *expr3*
PATH (*correlation_int*)	Returns the relative path to the resource specified in an UNDER_PATH or EQUALS_PATH condition
SYS_CONNECT_BY_PATH (*column,char*)	Returns the path of a column value from root to node in an hierarchical query. Column values are separated by *char*.

Table 1-10 Miscellaneous Single Row Functions (continued)

Function	What it does
SYS_CONTEXT('namespace', 'param'[,len])	Returns a VARCHAR2 with the value of param of namespace. Return is 256 bytes unless overridden by len.
SYS_DBURIGEN(collattr [rowid][,collattr [rowid],...] [,'text()'])	Generates a URL that can be used to retrieve an XML document from one or more columns col or attributes attr with or without a rowid
SYS_EXTRACT_UTC(time)	Returns the UTC from time where time is a datetime with time zone displacement
SYS_GUID()	Generates and then returns a Globally Unique IDentifier (GUID) of 16 RAW bytes
SYS_TYPEID(obj_val)	Returns the typeid of an object type operand
SYS_XMLAGG(expr [fmt])	Creates a single well-formed XML document from multiple documents
SYS_XMLGEN(expr [fmt])	Creates a well-formed XML document from a database row/column expression
UID	Returns the UID of the current session user
UPDATEXML(XML_instance, path, expr)	Updates an XML document by searching for the node specified in the path, then replaces either the node or the scalar value of the node, depending on argument types
USER	Returns the username of the current session user
USERENV(param)	Returns a variety of information about the current session. While deprecated in favor of SYS_CONTEXT, this is retained for backward compatibility.
VSIZE(expr)	Returns the number of bytes used by the value represented by expr
XMLAGG(XML_instance [ORDER BY sortlist])	Returns a well-formed XML document by aggregating a series of XML fragments. The returned document is a simple aggregate and no formatting is supported.

Table 1-10 Miscellaneous Single Row Functions (continued)

Function	What it does
XMLCOLATTVAL	Creates an XML fragment for one or more columns of a single row. The format of the fragment is fixed as <column name=" *column name* "> *column value* </column>.
XMLCONCAT(*XML_instance* [, *XML_instance,...*])	Returns an XML fragment created by concatenating a series of XML fragments or elements
XMLFOREST	Creates an XML fragment for one or more columns of a single row. The format of the fragment is fixed as <column name>column value</column name>.
XMLSEQUENCE	Used to "unroll" a stored XMLType into multiple rows for further processing as individual elements
XMLTRANSFORM	Applies an XSL style sheet to an XML document and returns the resulting new XML document

Aggregate Functions

All of the aggregate functions described below can have an analytical clause appended to them using the *OVER* (*analytical_clause*) syntax. For space considerations, we've omitted this from the **Function** column.

Table 1-11 Aggregate Functions

Function	What it does
AVG([*DISTINCT*|*ALL*] *expr*)	Computes the average of the rows returned by *expr*. If the DISTINCT keyword is used, duplicate rows will be excluded from the calculation.
CORR(*expr1* , *expr2*)	Calculates the coefficient of correlation between *expr1* and *expr2*
COUNT(* | [*DISTINCT*|*ALL*] *expr*)	Returns the number of [*DISTINCT*] rows in the *expr* that are not null, or if * is specified, the total number of rows, including duplicates and nulls

Table 1-11 Aggregate Functions (continued)

Function	What it does
COVAR_POP(*expr1, expr2*)	Given a set of pairs, *expr1* and *expr2*, where nulls are excluded, returns the population covariance
COVAR_SAMP(*expr1, expr2*)	Given a set of pairs, *expr1* and *expr2*, where nulls are excluded, returns the sample covariance
CUME_DIST(*expr[,expr...]*) *WITHIN GROUP* (*ORDER BY expr [DESC|ASC] [NULLS [FIRST|LAST]*)	Given a list of values, finds and returns the cumulative distribution of a single value within that list
DENSE_RANK(*expr[,expr...]*) *WITHIN GROUP* (*ORDER BY expr*)	Given an ordered group of rows, finds and returns the rank of a single value within that group
FIRST ORDER BY *expr [DESC|ASC] [NULLS [FIRST|LAST]*)	Returns the first row or rows from a set based on the specified sort order. If multiple rows tie as "first" then all tied rows will be returned. Used in an aggregate function.
GROUP_ID()	Used in GROUP BY specification to distinguish duplicate groups
GROUPING(*expr*)	Used to distinguish superaggregate rows from regular grouped rows when ROLLUP and CUBE are used
GROUPING_ID(*expr[,expr...]*)	Returns the number of the GROUPING bit vector for a row
LAST ORDER BY *expr [DESC|ASC] [NULLS [FIRST|LAST]*)	Returns the last row or rows from a set based on the specified sort order. If multiple rows tie as "last" then all tied rows will be returned. Used in an aggregate function.
MAX([*DISTINCT|ALL] expr*)	Returns the maximum value of *expr*. If the DISTINCT keyword is used, duplicate rows will be excluded from the calculation.
MIN([*DISTINCT|ALL] expr*)	Returns the minimum value of *expr*. If the DISTINCT keyword is used, duplicate rows will be excluded from the calculation.

Table 1-11 Aggregate Functions (continued)

Function	What it does
PERCENTILE_CONT(*expr*) WITHIN GROUP (ORDER BY *expr* [DESC|ASC])	Given a list of values and a specified percentile ranking, returns the interpolated value of that percentile by assuming a continuous distribution of data in the list
PERCENTILE_DISC(*expr*) WITHIN GROUP (ORDER BY *expr* [DESC|ASC])	Given a list of values and a specified percentile ranking, returns the smallest value that meets or exceeds that percentile rank by assuming a discrete distribution of data in the list
PERCENT_RANK(*expr*) WITHIN GROUP (ORDER BY *expr* [DESC|ASC]|NULLS FIRST|LAST])	Given a list of values, calculates the hypothetical rank of a single value within that list
RANK(*expr*) WITHIN GROUP (ORDER BY *expr* [DESC|ASC]|NULLS FIRST|LAST])	Returns the rank (ordering) of *expr* in the group of values returned by the *order* by expression
STDDEV([DISTINCT|ALL] expr)	Returns the standard deviation of *expr*
STDDEV_POP([DISTINCT|ALL] expr)	Returns the square root of the population variance from computing the standard deviation of *expr*
STDDEV_SAMP([DISTINCT|ALL] expr)	Returns the square root of the cumulative sample standard deviation of *expr*
SUM([DISTINCT|ALL] expr)	Returns the sum of *expr*. Distinct eliminates duplicates from the set of values being summed.
VAR_POP(*expr*)	Returns the population variance of *expr*. Nulls are removed from the calculation.
VAR_SAMP(*expr*)	Returns the sample variance of *expr*. Nulls are removed from the calculation.
VARIANCE([DISTINCT|ALL] expr)	The variance of *expr*, with duplicates removed if *DISTINCT* is specified

Table 1-12   Regression Functions

Function	What it does
REGR_SLOPE(*expr,expr2*)	Returns the slope of a least squares regression line of the set of number pairs defined by (*expr,expr2*)
REGR_INTERCEPT(*expr,expr2*)	Returns the Y intercept of a least squares regression line of the set of number pairs defined by (*expr,expr2*)
REGR_COUNT(*expr,expr2*)	Returns the number of NOT NULL pairs used to fit the least squares regression line of the set of number pairs defined by (*expr,expr2*)
REGR_R2(*expr,expr2*)	Returns the R^2 value (coefficient of determination) of a least squares regression line of the set of number pairs defined by (*expr,expr2*)
REGR_AVGX(*expr,expr2*)	Returns the average value of *expr2* of a least squares regression line of the set of number pairs defined by (*expr,expr2*) after removing nulls from the calculation
REGR_AVGY(*expr,expr2*)	Returns the average value of *expr* of a least squares regression line of the set of number pairs defined by (*expr,expr2*) after removing nulls from the calculation
REGR_SXX(*expr,expr2*)	Returns the value of calculating REGR_COUNT(*expr, expr2*) * VAR_POP(*expr2*) with nulls removed from the calculation
REGR_SYY(*expr,expr2*)	Returns the value of calculating REGR_COUNT(*expr, expr2*) * VAR_POP(*expr*) with nulls removed from the calculation
REGR_SXY(*expr,expr2*)	Returns the value of calculating REGR_COUNT(*expr, expr2*) * COVAR_POP(*expr,expr2*) with nulls removed from the calculation

Analytical Functions

All of the aggregate functions described above can also have analytic functionality, using the OVER (*analytical_clause*) syntax. For space considerations, we've declined to list them twice. Note that you cannot nest analytic functions.

Table 1-13   Analytical Functions

Function	What it does
FIRST_VALUE(*expr*) OVER (*analytical_clause*)	Returns the first in the ordered set of *expr*
LAG(*expr*[,*offset*][,*default*]) OVER (*analytical_clause*)	Provides access at a point *offset* prior to the cursor in a series of rows returned by *expr*
LAST_VALUE(*expr*) OVER (*analytical_clause*)	Returns the last in the ordered set of *expr*
LEAD(*expr*[,*offset*][,*default*]) OVER (*analytical_clause*)	Provides access at a point *offset* beyond the cursor in a series of rows returned by *expr*
NTILE(*expr*) OVER (*analytical_clause*)	Divides the ordered dataset into *expr* number of buckets
RATIO_TO_REPORT(*expr*) OVER (*analytical_clause*)	Returns the ratio of *expr* to the sum returned by *analytical_clause*
ROW_NUMBER(*expr*) OVER ([*partition_clause*]*order_by_clause*)	Assigns a unique number to each row

Object Reference Functions

Table 1-14 Object Reference Functions

Function	What it does
DEREF(*expr*)	Returns the object reference of *expr*. Without this, an the object ID of the reference would be returned.
MAKE_REF(*table|view,key [,key...]*)	Returns a REF to a row of an object view or table
REF(*correlation_var*)	Returns the REF value of *correlation_var*
REFTOHEX(*expr*)	Converts *expr* to its hexadecimal equivalent where *expr* is a REF
VALUE(*correlation_var*)	Returns the value associated with the *correlation_var*

FORMAT MODELS

Date Format Models

Table 1-15 Date Format Models

Element	Value Returned
- / . ; "text"	Quoted text and punctuation are reproduced in the result
AD A.D.	Indicates date that is AD. Periods optional
AM A.M. PM P.M.	Before or after noon. Periods optional
BC B.C.	Indicates date that is BC. Periods optional
CC SCC	Century (SCC precedes BC century with -)
D	The day of week (1–7)

Table 1-15 Date Format Models (continued)

Element	Value Returned
DAY	The name of the day of the week (Monday, Tuesday, etc.). Padded to 9 characters.
DD	Day of month (1–31)
DDD	The number of the day of year (1–366)
DY	The name of the day of the week, abbreviated
E	Abbreviated era name (for Japanese Imperial, ROC Official, and Thai Buddha calendars)
EE	Full era name
FF [1–9]	Fractional seconds. 1–9 specifies the number of digits
HH	Hour of day(12-hour clock)
HH12	Hour of day (12-hour clock)
HH24	Hour of day (24-hour clock)
IW	Number of Week of the year
IYY IY I	Last 3, 2, or 1 digit(s) of ISO year
IYYY	4-digit ISO year
J	Julian day(number of days since January 1, 4712 BC)
MI	Minute (0–59)
MM	Month (01–12)
MON	JAN, FEB, MAR, etc.
MONTH	Full month name, padded to 9 characters
Q	Quarter of year where JAN–MAR = 1
RM	Month in Roman numerals (I–XII; JAN = I)

Table 1-15 Date Format Models (continued)

Element	Value Returned
RR	Last two digits of the year, for years in previous or next century (where previous if current year is <=50, next if current year >50)
RRRR	Round year. Accepts 4 or 2 digit input, 2 digit returns as RR.
SS	Seconds (0–59)
SSSSS	Seconds past midnight (0–86399)
TZD	Abbreviated Time Zone String with Daylight Savings
TZH	Time zone hour
TZM	Time zone minute
WW	The week of the year (1–53)
W	The week of the month
X	Local radix character
Y, YYY	Year, with comma as shown
YEAR SYEAR	Year, fully spelled out. For SYEAR, BC dates use "-"
Y YY YYY	Final one, two, or three digits of the year

Date Prefixes and Suffixes

The following prefixes can be added to date formats:

FM	The fill mode toggle. Suppresses blank padding of MONTH or DAY
FX	Specifies that the format of TO_DATE functions must be an exact match

The following suffixes may be added to date formats:

TH	converts to an ordinal number ("5TH")
SP	Spells out the number ("FIVE")
SPTH or THSP	Spells out the ordinal number ("FIFTH")

Number Format Models

Table 1-16 Number Format Models

Element	Example	Value Returned
,	9,999	Returns a comma at the position specified
.	99.99	Returns a period (decimal point) at the position specified
$	$9999	Leading dollar sign
0	0999	Returns value with leading zeros
0	9990	Returns value with trailing zeros
9	9999	Returns value with the specified number of digits. Leading space if positive, − if negative. Leading zeros are blank, except when integer portion is zero, then a single leading zero is returned.
B	B9999	As in 9, above, but returns a blank in all cases for leading zeros
C	C999	Returns the ISO currency symbol
D	99D99	Returns the NLS decimal character in the specified position
EEEE	9.9EEEE	Returns value in scientific notation

Table 1-16 Number Format Models (continued)

Element	Example	Value Returned
FM	FM90.9	Returns a value without leading or trailing blanks
G	9G999	Returns the value with the NLS group separator in the specified position
L	L999	Returns the value with the NLS Local Currency Symbol in the specified position. Negative values have a trailing minus sign (–), positive values with a trailing blank.
PR	9999PR	Returns negative values in <angle brackets>, positives have leading and trailing blanks
RN rn	RN rn	Returns the value as Roman numerals, in the case-specified
S	S9999 9999S	Returns the value with a + or – sign denoting positive or negative value in the position shown (can only be first or last position).
TM	TM	"Text minimum." Returns the smallest number of characters possible and is case-insensitive. Default is TM9 that uses fixed notation up to 64 characters, then scientific notation.
U	U9999	Returns the "Euro" (or other) NLS dual currency symbol in the specified position
V	999V99	Returns a value multiplied by 10 times the number of 9s specified after the V
X	XXXX	Returns the Hexadecimal value. Precede with a 0 to have leading zeros, or FM to remove the leading blank.

RESERVED WORDS

The following are the reserved words in Oracle SQL. Those in *italics* are also ANSI reserved words. In addition, Oracle uses the "SYS_" prefix internally to identify implicitly generated schema objects and you should avoid the use of any words beginning with this prefix.

ACCESS	*CREATE*	*HAVING*	MODE	*PUBLIC*	SYSDATE
ADD	*CURRENT*	IDENTIFIED	MODIFY	RAW	*TABLE*
ALL	*DATE*	*IMMEDIATE*	NOAUDIT	RENAME	*THEN*
ALTER	*DECIMAL*	*IN*	NOCOMPRESS	RESOURCE	*TO*
AND	*DEFAULT*	INCREMENT	*NOT*	*REVOKE*	TRIGGER
ANY	*DELETE*	INDEX	NOWAIT	ROW	UID
AS	*DESC*	INITIAL	*NULL*	ROWID	*UNION*
ASC	*DISTINCT*	*INSERT*	NUMBER	ROWNUM	*UNIQUE*
AUDIT	*DROP*	*INTEGER*	*OF*	*ROWS*	*UPDATE*
BETWEEN	*ELSE*	*INTERSECT*	OFFLINE	*SELECT*	*USER*
BY	EXCLUSIVE	*INTO*	*ON*	*SESSION*	VALIDATE
CHAR	EXISTS	*IS*	ONLINE	*SET*	*VALUES*
CHECK	FILE	*LEVEL*	*OPTION*	SHARE	*VARCHAR*
CLUSTER	*FLOAT*	*LIKE*	*OR*	*SIZE*	VARCHAR2
COLUMN	*FOR*	LOCK	*ORDER*	*SMALLINT*	*VIEW*
COMMENT	*FROM*	LONG	PCTFREE	START	*WHENEVER*
COMPRESS	*GRANT*	MAXEXTENTS	*PRIOR*	SUCCESSFUL	*WHERE*
CONNECT	*GROUP*	MINUS	*PRIVILEGES*	SYNONYM	*WITH*

PRIVILEGES

Oracle supports a rich selection of privileges that are assigned with the GRANT command, and removed with the REVOKE command.

System Privileges

System privileges are granted and revoked to users and roles and generally apply to an entire class or group of objects. To be able to GRANT or REVOKE a system privilege, the user must have been granted the privilege with the ADMIN OPTION, or have the GRANT ANY PRIVILEGE system privilege.

Table 1-17   System Privileges

Class	Privilege	Applies To
Clusters	Create Cluster	A cluster in its own schema
	Create Any Cluster	Any cluster in any schema
	Alter Any Cluster	Any cluster in any schema
	Drop Any Cluster	Any cluster in any schema
Contexts	Create Any Context	Any context namespace
	Drop Any Context	Any context namespace
Database	Alter Database	The database
	Alter System	ALTER SYSTEM statements
	Audit System	AUDIT *sql* statements

Table 1-17   System Privileges (continued)

Class	Privilege	Applies To
Database Links	Create Database Link	Private links in own schema
	Create Public Database Links	Public database links
	Drop Public Database Links	Public database links
Debugging	Debug Connect Session	Current Session can be connected to a JDWP (Java Debug Wire Protocol) debugger
	Debug Any Procedure	All PL/SQL and Java code in any database object
Dimensions	Create Dimension	Dimensions in own schema
	Create Any Dimension	Dimensions in any schema
	Alter Any Dimension	Dimensions in any schema
	Drop Any Dimension	Dimensions in any schema
Directories	Create Any Directory	Directory database objects
	Drop Any Directory	Directory database objects
Indextypes	Create Indextype	Indextypes in own schema
	Create Any Indextype	Indextypes in any schema
	Alter Any Indextype	Indextypes in any schema
	Drop Any Indextype	Indextypes in any schema
	Execute Any Indextype	Indextypes in any schema

Table 1-17 System Privileges (continued)

Class	Privilege	Applies To
Indexes	Create Any Index	Any table in any schema or a domain index in any schema
	Alter Any Index	Any schema
	Drop Any Index	Any schema
	Query Rewrite	Materialized views or function-based index in own schema
	Global Query Rewrite	Materialized views or function-based index in any schema
Libraries	Create Library	External procedure or function library in own schema
	Create Any Library	External procedure or function library in any schema
	Drop Any Library	External procedure or function library in any schema
Materialized Views	Create Materialized View	Materialized view in own schema
	Create Any Materialized View	Materialized view in any schema
	Alter Any Materialized View	Materialized view in any schema
	Drop Any Materialized View	Materialized view in any schema
	Query Rewrite	Materialized views or function-based index in own schema
	Global Query Rewrite	Materialized views or function-based index in any schema
	On Commit Refresh	Create a refresh on commit materialized view or alter a refresh on demand materialized view on any table in database
	Flashback Any Table	Any table, view, or materialized view in the database

Table 1-17   System Privileges (continued)

Class	Privilege	Applies To
Operators	Create Operator	Operator in own schema
	Create Any Operator	Operator in any schema
	Drop Any Operator	Operator in any schema
	Execute Any Operator	Operator in any schema
Outlines	Create Any Outline	Public outlines in any schema
	Alter Any Outline	Public outlines in any schema
	Alter Any Outline	Public outlines in any schema
	Select Any Outline	Create a private outline that is a clone of a public one
Procedures	Create Procedure	Stored procedures, functions, and packages in own schema
	Create Any Procedure	Stored procedures, functions, and packages in any schema
	Alter Any Procedure	Stored procedures, functions, and packages in any schema
	Drop Any Procedure	Stored procedures, functions, and packages in any schema
	Execute Any Procedure	Stored procedures, functions, and packages in any schema
Profiles	Create Profile	Profiles
	Alter Profile	Profiles
	Drop Profile	Profiles

Table 1-17 System Privileges (continued)

Class	Privilege	Applies To
Roles	Create Role	Create new roles
	Alter Any Role	Any role in the database
	Drop Any Role	Any role in the database
	Grant Any Role	Any role in the database
Rollback Segments	Create Rollback Segment	Rollback segments
	Alter Rollback Segments	Rollback segments
	Drop Rollback Segments	Rollback segments
Sequences	Create Sequence	Sequences in own schema
	Create Any Sequence	Sequences in any schema
	Alter Any Sequence	Sequences in any schema
	Drop Any Sequence	Sequences in any schema
	Select Any Sequence	Sequences in any schema
Sessions	Create Session	Connect to database
	Alter Resource Cost	Set resource costs for sessions
	Alter Session	Alter your current session parameters
	Restricted Session	Connect to database when RESTRICTED SESSION is in effect

Table 1-17 System Privileges (continued)

Class	Privilege	Applies To
Synonym	Create Synonym	Synonyms in own schema
	Create Any Synonym	Private synonyms in any schema
	Drop Any Synonym	Private synonyms in any schema
	Create Public Synonym	Public synonyms
	Drop Public Synonym	Public synonyms
Tables	Create Table	Tables in own schema
	Create Any Table	Tables in any schema
	Alter Any Table	Tables or views in any schema
	Back Up Any Table	Export objects from any schema
	Delete Any Table	Rows from tables, views, or table partitions in any schema
	Drop Any Table	Tables or table partitions in any schema (includes TRUNCATE)
	Insert Any Table	Rows into any table or view in any schema
	Lock Any Table	Tables or views in any schema
	Select Any Table	Tables or views in any schema
	Flashback Any Table	Any table, view, or materialized view in the database
	Update Any Table	Rows in any table or view in any schema

Table 1-17 System Privileges (continued)

Class	Privilege	Applies To
Tablespaces	Create Tablespace	Tablespaces
	Alter Tablespace	Tablespaces
	Drop Tablespace	Tablespaces
	Manage Tablespaces	Online and offline of tablespaces and begin or end backups of tablespaces
	Unlimited Tablespace	Unlimited storage on any tablespace. Overrides specific quotas
Triggers	Create Trigger	Triggers in own schema
	Create Any Trigger	Triggers in any schema
	Alter Any Trigger	Triggers in any schema
	Drop Any Trigger	Triggers in any schema
	Administer Database Trigger	Create trigger on database. Also requires Create Trigger or Create Any Trigger.
Types	Create Type	Object types and bodies in own schema
	Create Any Type	Object types and bodies in any schema
	Alter Any Type	Object types and bodies in any schema
	Drop Any Type	Object types and bodies in any schema
	Execute Any Type	Object types and bodies in any schema
	Under Any Type	Create subtypes

Table 1-17 System Privileges (continued)

Class	Privilege	Applies To
Users	Create User	Create users. Implicitly allows the setting of passwords, quotas, default, and temporary tablespaces and assigning of profiles for new users.
	Alter User	Alter settings for existing users. Implicitly allows the setting of passwords, quotas, default, and temporary tablespaces and assigning of profiles.
	Become User	Change to any other user (required for full database imports)
	Drop User	Drop any user
Views	Create View	Views in own schema
	Create Any View	Views in any schema
	Drop Any View	Views in any schema
	Under Any View	Create subviews of any view
	Flashback Any Table	Any table, view, or materialized view in the database
Miscellaneous	Analyze Any	Any table, cluster, or index in any schema
	Audit Any	Any object in any schema
	Comment Any Table	Any table, view, or column in any schema
	Exempt Access Policy	Bypass access control
	Force Transaction	Own in-doubt distributed transactions
	Force Any Transaction	Force the commit or rollback of any in-doubt distributed transaction

Table 1-17 System Privileges *(continued)*

Class	Privilege	Applies To
	Grant Any Object Privilege	Grant or revoke any object privilege
	Grant Any Privilege	Grant any system privilege
	Resumable	Enable resumable allocation of space
	Select Any Dictionary	Query SYS data dictionary objects. Overrides an init parameter of FALSE to 07_DICTIONARY_ACCESSIBILITY.
	SYSDBA	STARTUP and SHUTDOWN, ALTER DATABASE, CREATE DATABASE, ARCHIVELOG, RECOVERY, CREATE SPFILE, RESTRICTED SESSION
	SYSOPER	Similar to SYSDBA, but can't create a database, and can't change the character set

Warning The grant of an ANY privilege gives the grantee the rights to that type of object in ALL schemas, including SYS, unless the database is started with an init parameter of:
07_DICTIONARY_ACCESSIBILITY = FALSE
When this parameter is set to FALSE, the ANY privilege applies to all schemas except SYS.

Object Privileges

In addition to System Privileges, Oracle supports assignment of privileges at the object level as well.

Table 1-18   Object Privileges

Privilege	Object	Explanation
Alter	Table	Modify the table definitions
	Sequence	Modify the sequence definition
Debug	Table	Use debugger on PL/SQL triggers on the table and SQL statements that reference the table
	View	Use debugger on PL/SQL triggers on the view and SQL statements that reference the view
	Procedures, Functions, and Packages	Use debugger to access all variables, methods, and types. Place breakpoints and stops.
Delete	Table	Delete rows
	View	Delete rows in the view
	Materialized View	Delete rows in the materialized view
Execute	Procedures, Functions, and Packages	Compile, or access public variables, methods and types through a debugger. Not required for indirect execution of the Procedure, function, or package.
	Library	Use the library and invoke its methods
	Operator	Reference the operator
	Indextype	Reference the Indextype

Table 1-18 Object Privileges (continued)

Privilege	Object	Explanation
Flashback	Table	Issue a flashback query on the table
	View	Issue a flashback query on the view
	Materialized View	Issue a flashback query on the materialized view
Index	Table	Create indices on the table
Insert	Table	Add rows to the table
	View	Add rows to the view
	Materialized View	Add rows to the materialized view
On Commit Refresh	Table	Create a materialized refresh on commit on the table. (Note: the privilege is on the table, not on the resultant view.)
Query Rewrite	Table	Create a materialized view on the table for Query Rewrite. (Note: the privilege is on the table, not on the resultant view.)
Read	Directory	Gives read permission on files stored on the operating system directory referenced
References	Table	Create a constraint that references the table
	View	Create foreign key constraints that reference the view

Table 1-18 Object Privileges (continued)

Privilege	Object	Explanation
Select	Table	Query the table. (You will need this privilege in addition to UPDATE and DELETE privileges if the database you're modifying is on a remote database.)
	View	Query the view
	Sequence	Get and increment the value of the sequence
	Materialized View	Query the materialized view
Under	View	Create subviews of the view
Update	Table	Modify data in the table using the UPDATE statement
	View	Modify data in the view
	Materialized View	Modify the data in the materialized view
Write	Directory	Gives write permission into the operating system directory referenced

Chapter Two

SQL Command Reference

ALTER

Alter statements modify the object referenced. The object must already exist.

Alter Cluster

Change storage for an existing cluster.

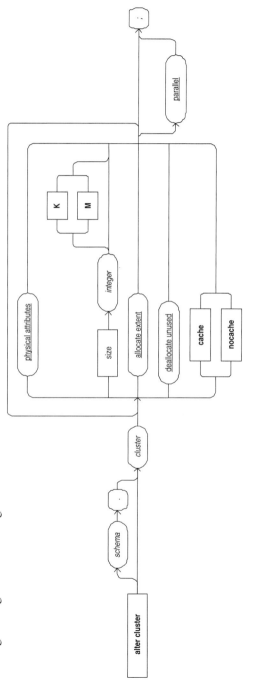

Alter Database

Alter the status, control files, redo logs, etc., of the database.

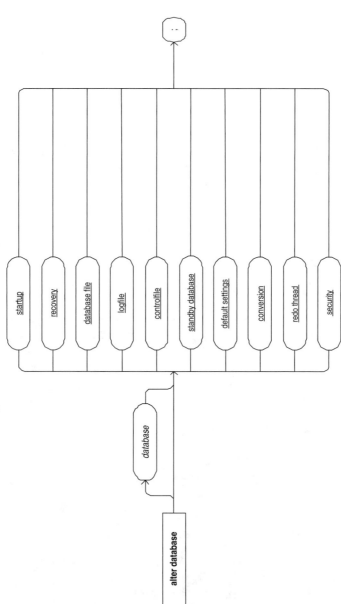

Startup

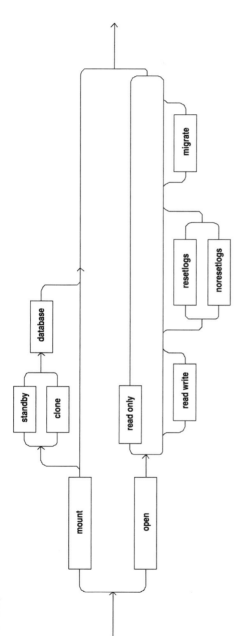

Recovery

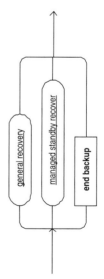

General recovery

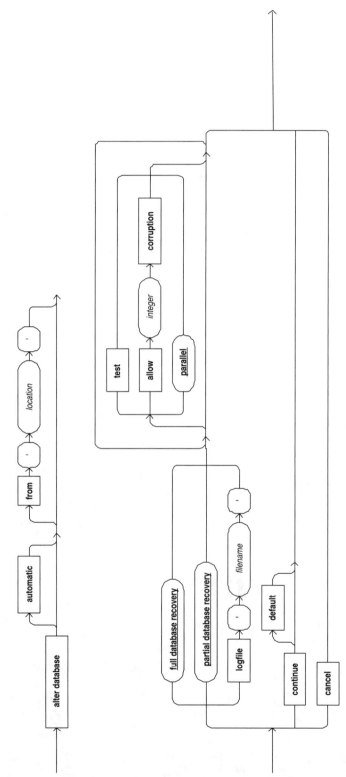

Full database recovery

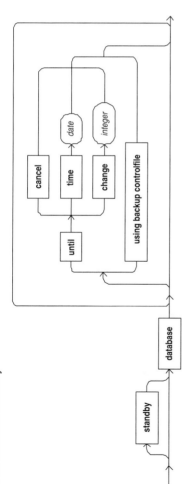

Partial database recovery

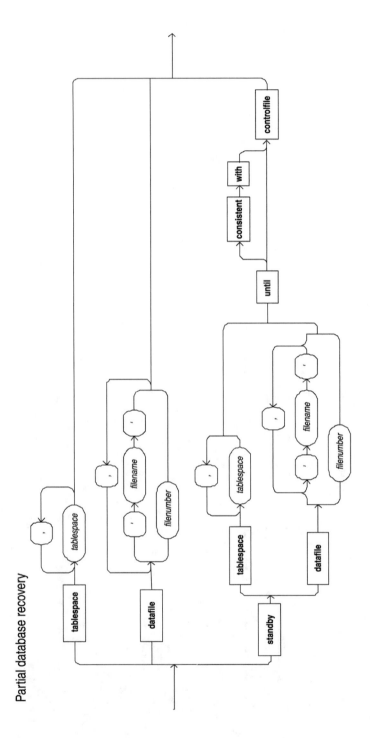

Parallel

Managed standby recovery

Recover

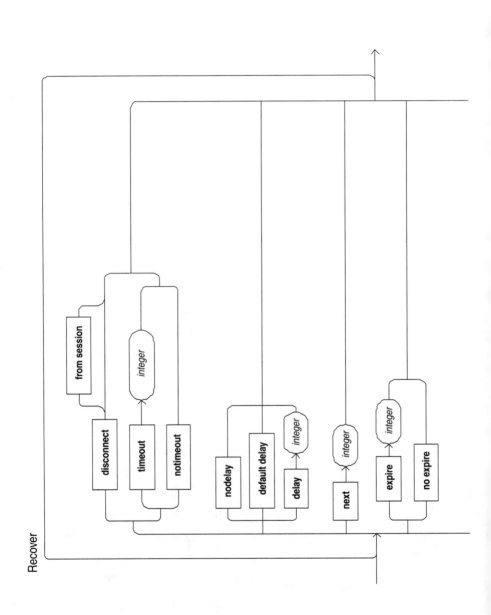

Recover (cont.)

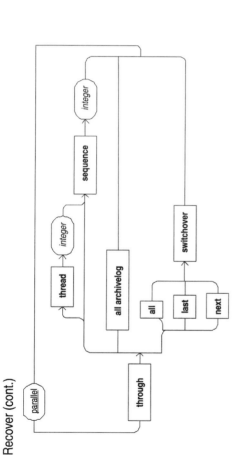

Cancel

Finish

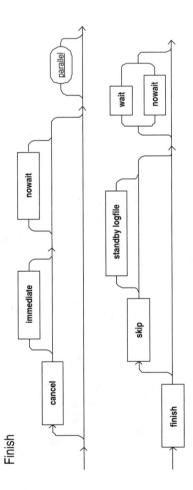

Database file

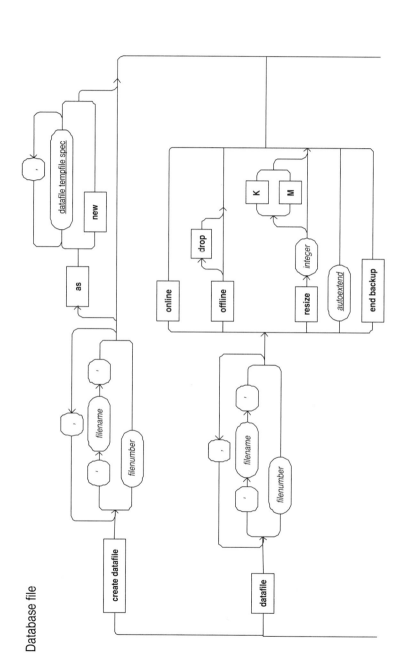

Database file (cont.)

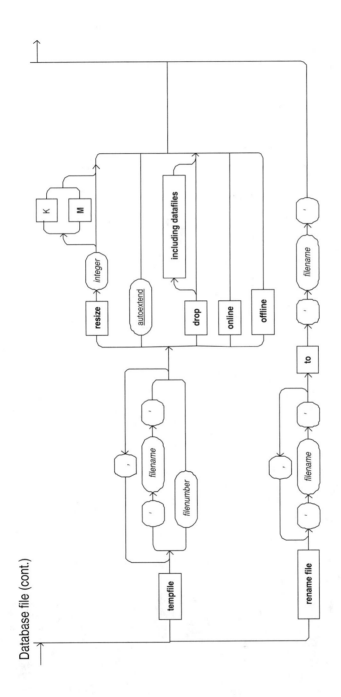

Autoextend

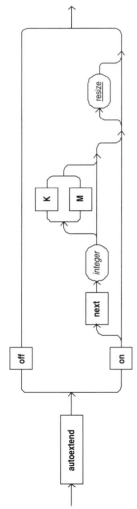

Maxsize

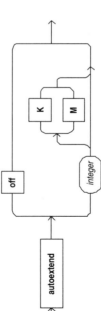

logfile

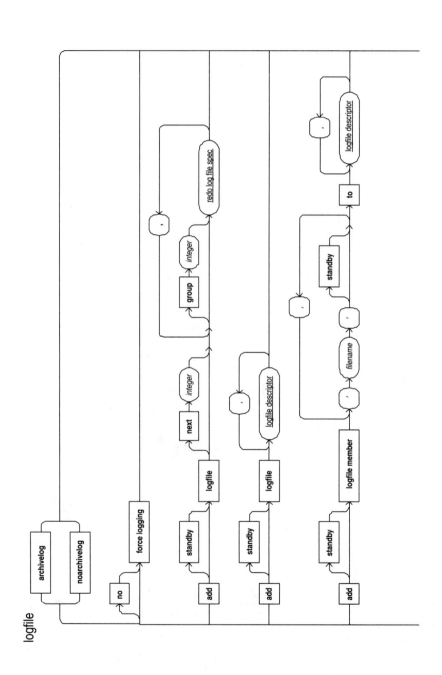

logfile (cont.)

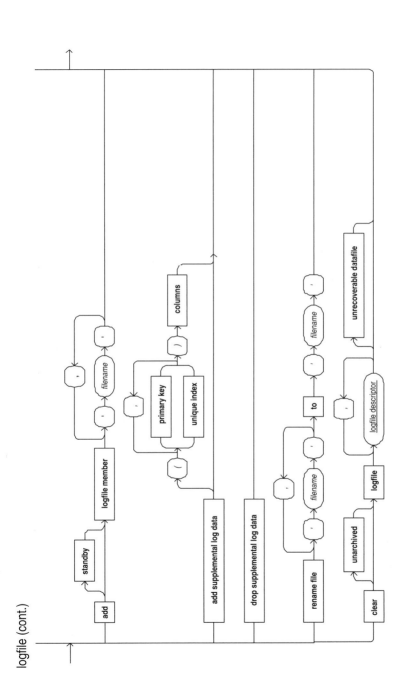

logfile descriptor

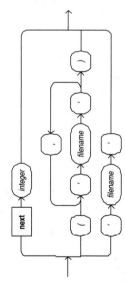

Controlfile

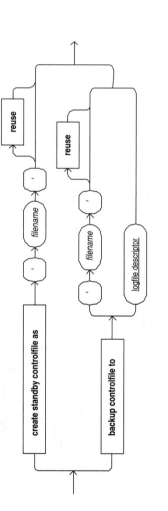

Trace file

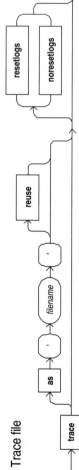

Standby database

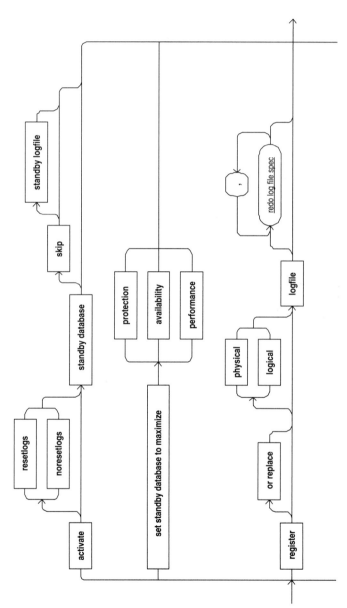

Standby database (cont.)

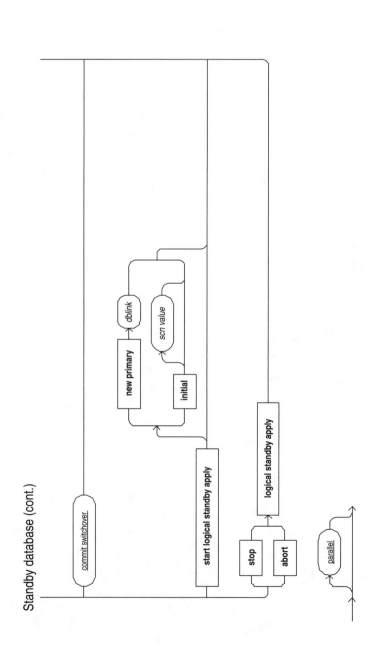

Commit switchover

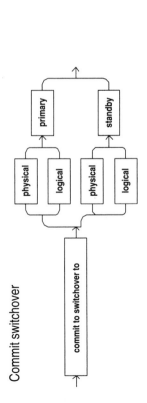

Default settings

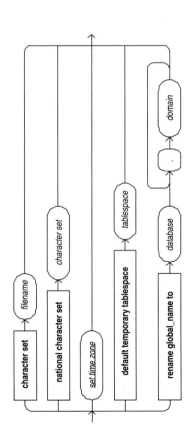

Set time_zone

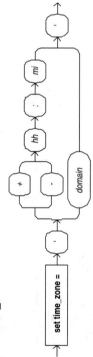

Conversion

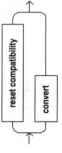

Redo thread

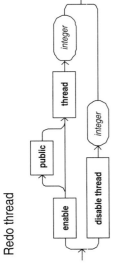

Security

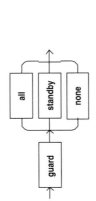

Alter Dimension

Modify the attributes or hierarchical relationships of a dimension.

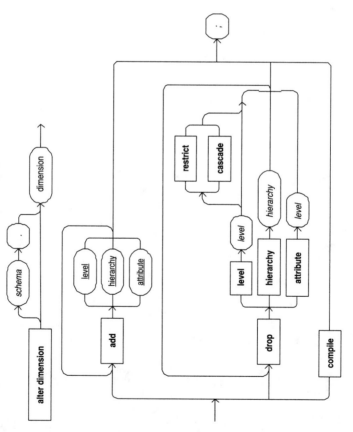

Level

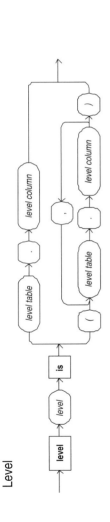

Hierarchy

Join

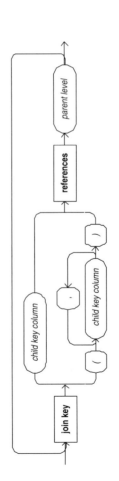

Attribute

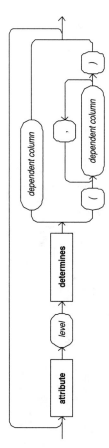

Alter Function

Recompile the function.

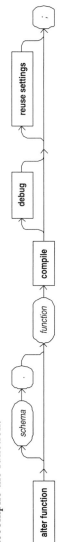

Alter Index

Modify storage for an existing index.

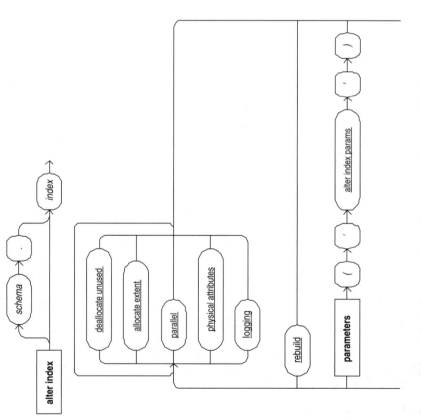

Alter Index (cont.)

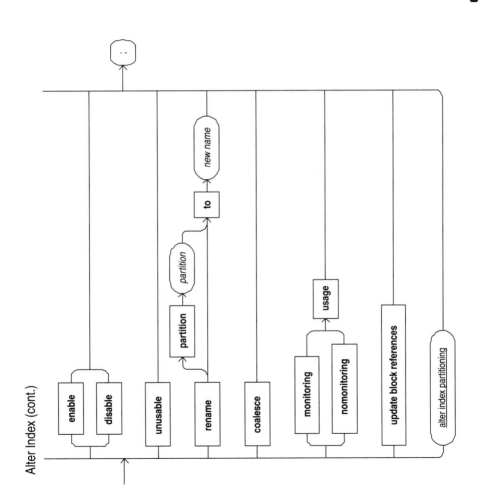

Rebuild

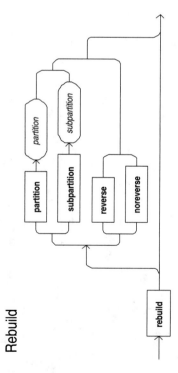

Rebuild (cont.)

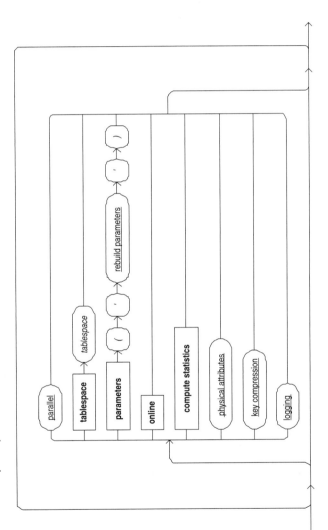

Key compression

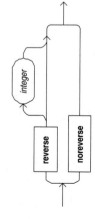

Alter index partitioning

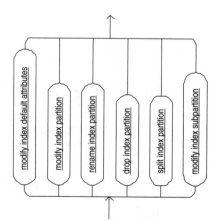

Modify index default attributes

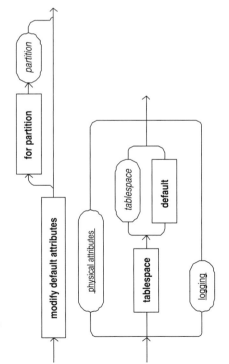

Modify index partition

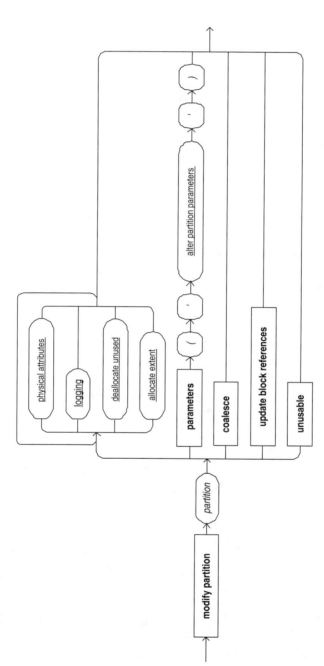

Rename index partition

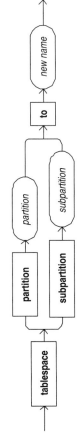

Drop index partition

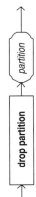

Split index partition

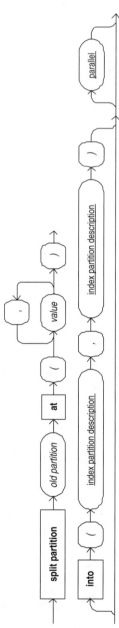

Index partition description

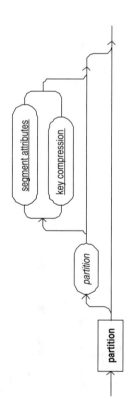

Segment attributes

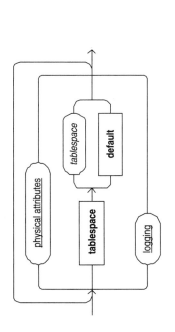

Modify index subpartition

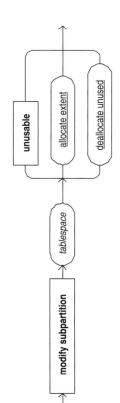

Alter Indextype

Modify the properties of the Indextype and add or drop operators.

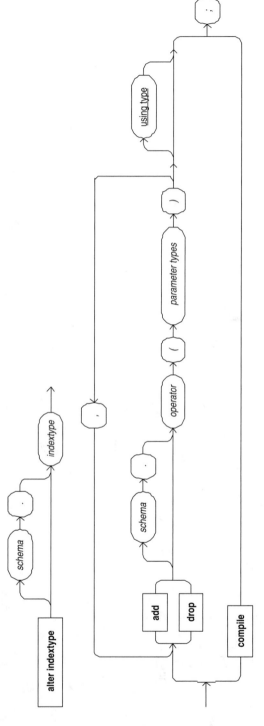

Using type

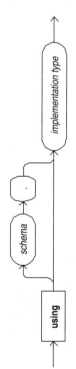

Alter Java

Force resolution of class schema objects and compilation of Java source schema objects.

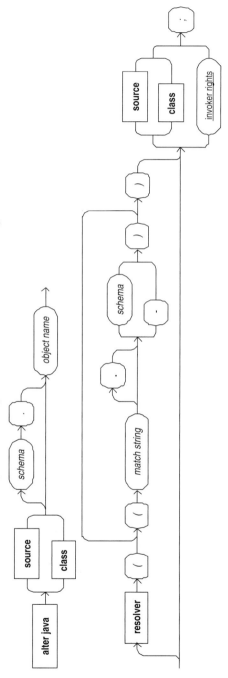

Invoker rights

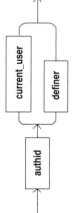

Alter Materialized View

Modify an existing Materialized View.

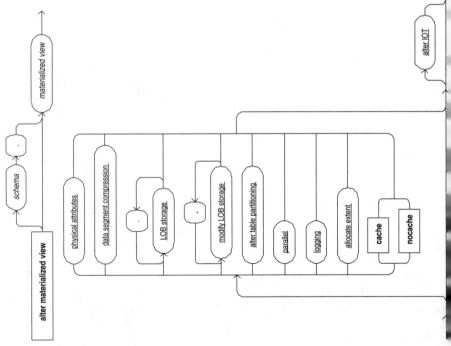

Alter Materialized View (cont.)

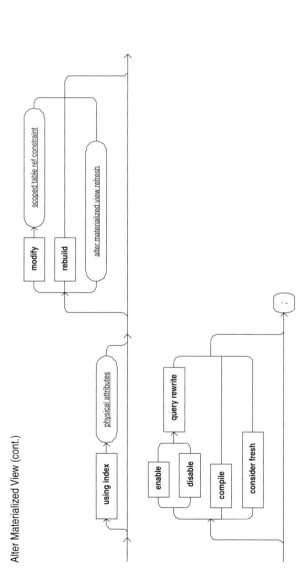

Data segment compression

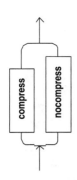

LOB storage

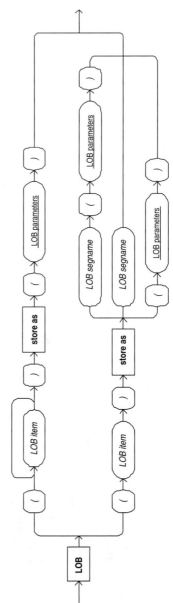

LOB parameters

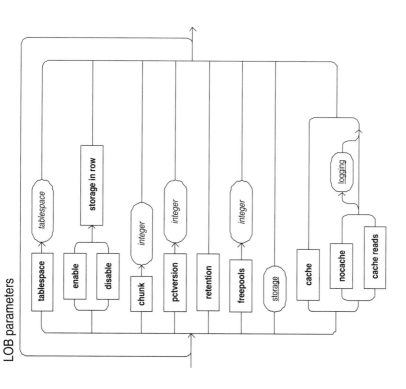

Modify LOB storage

Modify LOB parameters

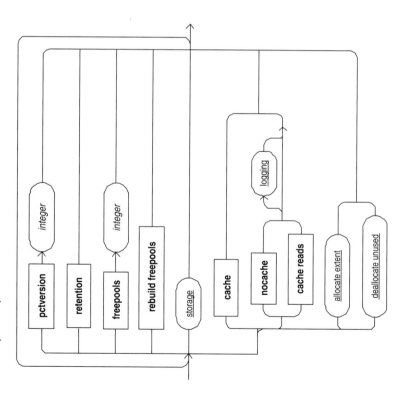

Alter IOT

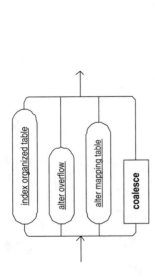

Index organized table

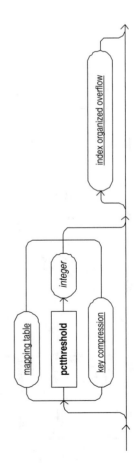

Index organized overflow

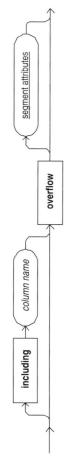

Alter overflow

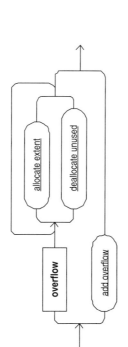

Add overflow

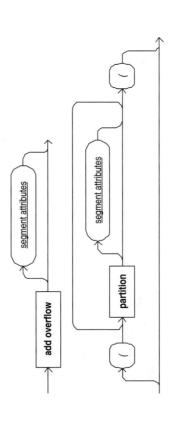

Scoped table ref constraint

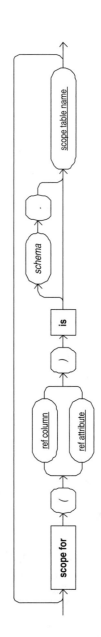

Alter materialized view refresh

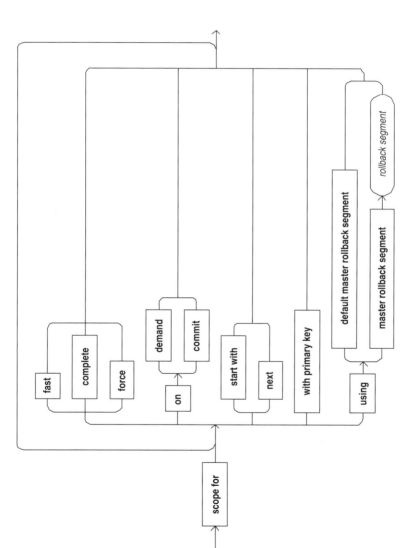

Alter materialized view refresh (cont.)

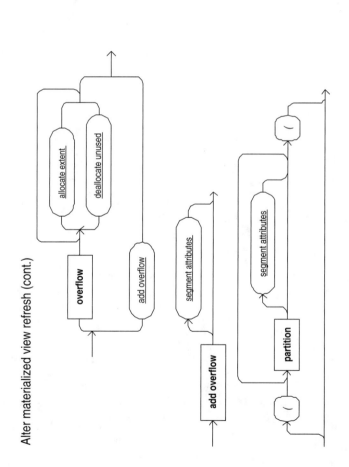

Alter Materialized View Log

Modify the characteristics of a Materialized View Log.

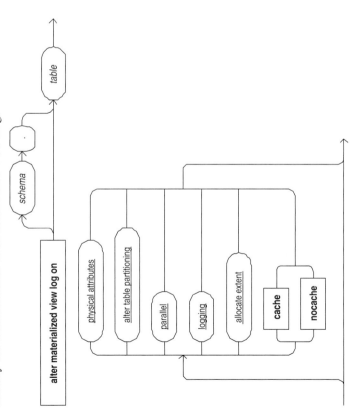

After materialized view (cont.)

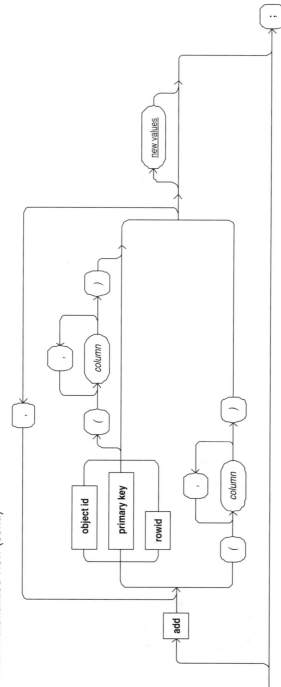

New values

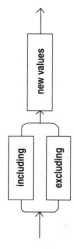

Alter Operator

Compile an existing operator.

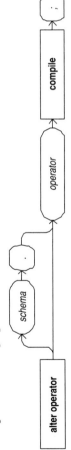

Alter Outline

Modify an existing outline statement.

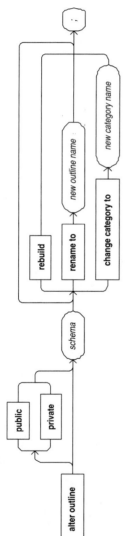

Alter Package

Recompile a package as a unit.

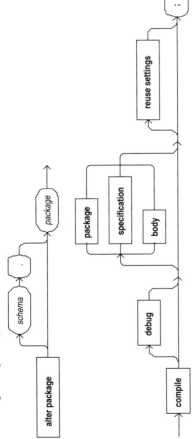

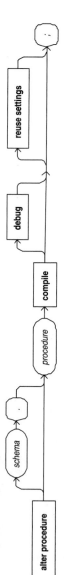

Alter Procedure

Recompile a standalone stored procedure.

Alter Profile

Modify a profile to change resource limits or password management in an existing profile.

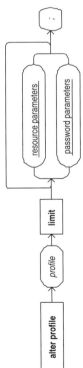

Resource parameters

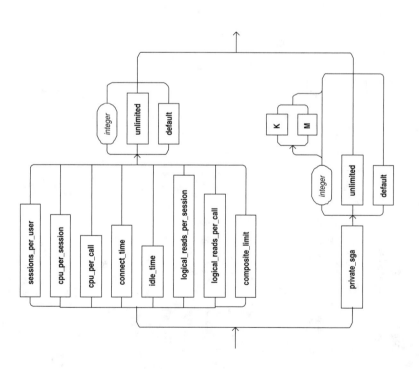

Password parameters

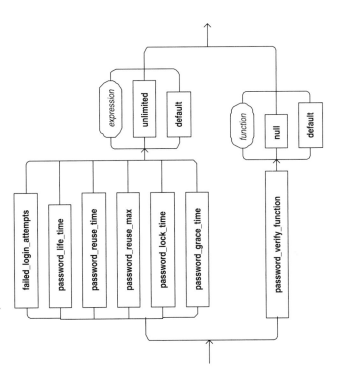

Alter Resource Cost

Specify or modify the resource cost for a particular session.

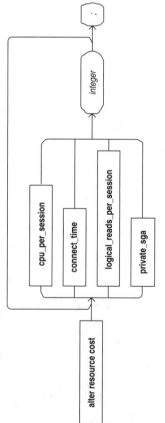

Alter Role

Modify the authorization parameters for a role.

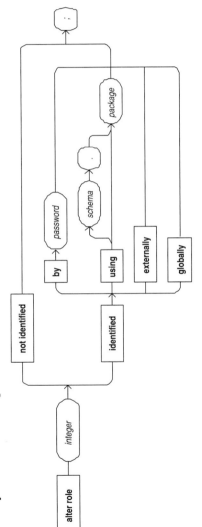

Alter Rollback Segment

Modify the status and storage parameters of a rollback segment.

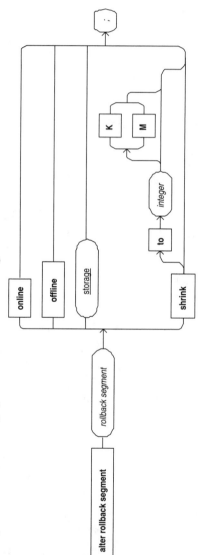

Alter Sequence

Modify the parameters of a sequence.

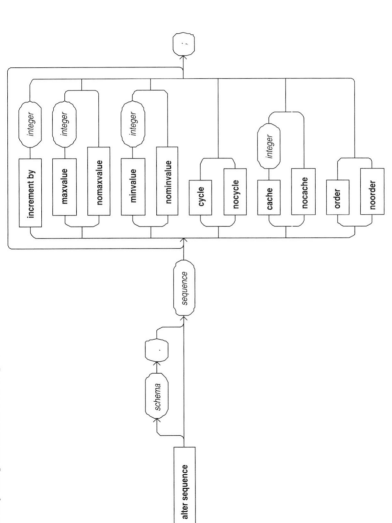

Alter Session

Modify the parameters of the current session.

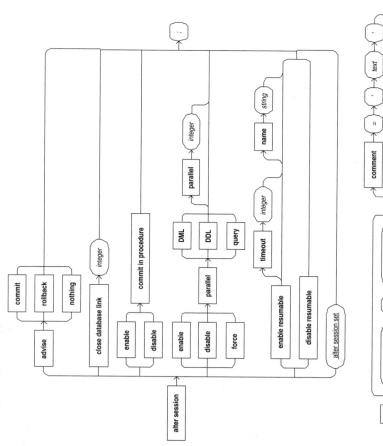

Alter System

Modify the parameters of the current instance, dynamically.

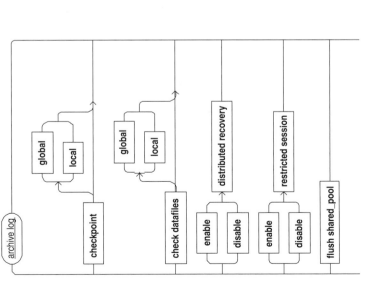

Alter System (cont.)

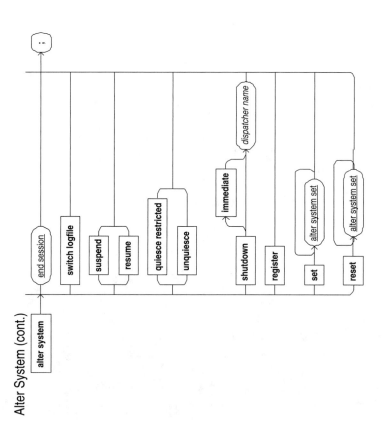

Archive log

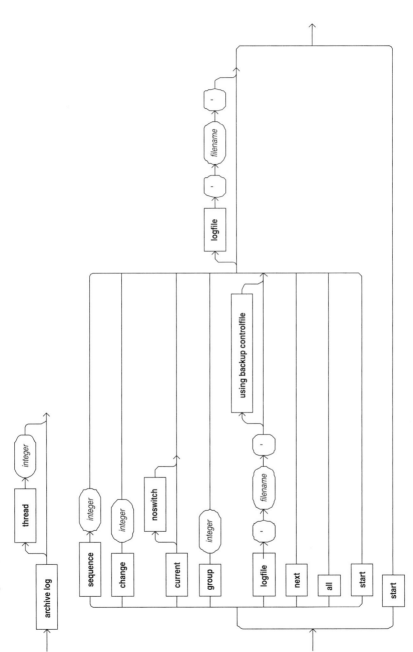

End session

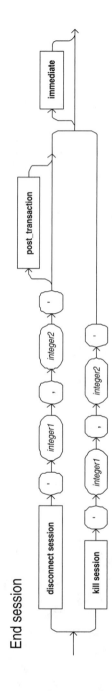

Alter system set

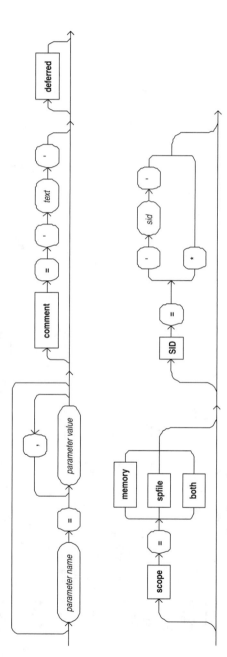

Alter system set

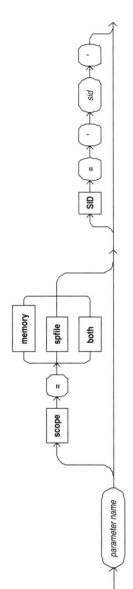

Alter Table

Alter the definition of a table, partitioned table, or table subpartition.

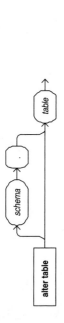

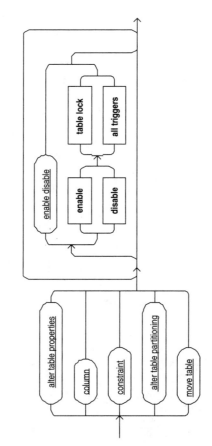

Alter table properties

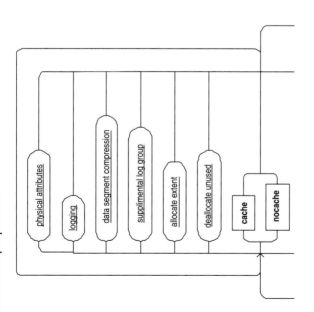

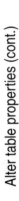

Alter table properties (cont.)

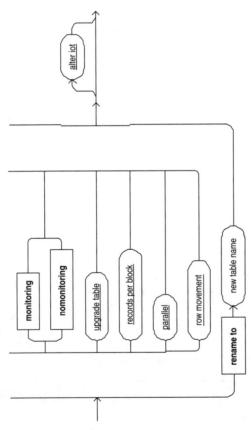

Data segment compression

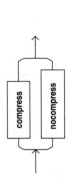

Supplemental log group

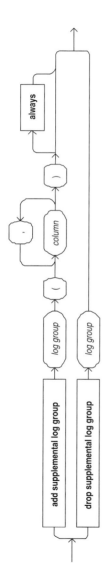

Upgrade table

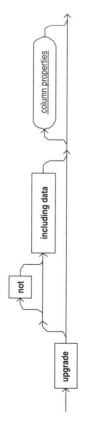

Records per block

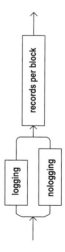

Row movement

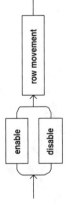

Alter IOT

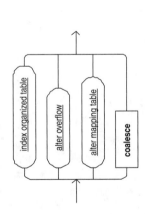

Index organized table

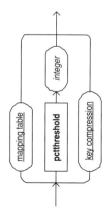

Mapping table

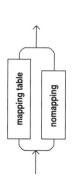

Key compression

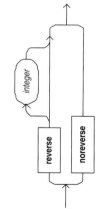

Index organized overflow

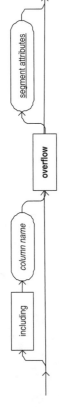

Segment attributes

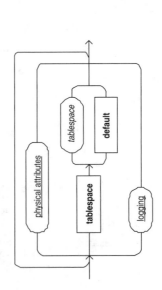

Alter overflow

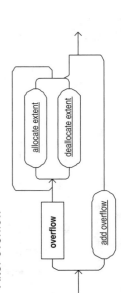

Add overflow

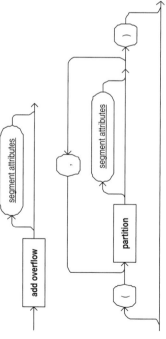

Alter mapping table

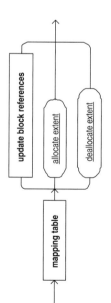

Column

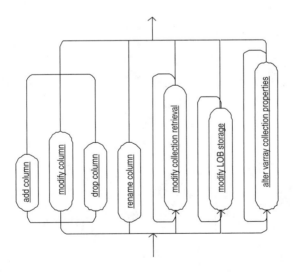

Add column

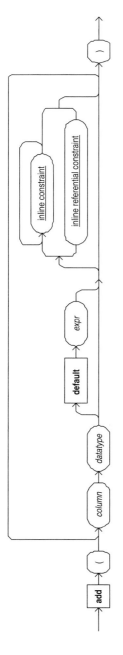

Modify column

Modify column properties

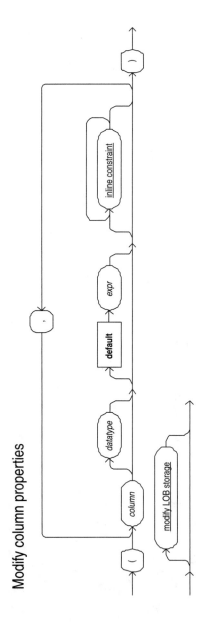

Drop column

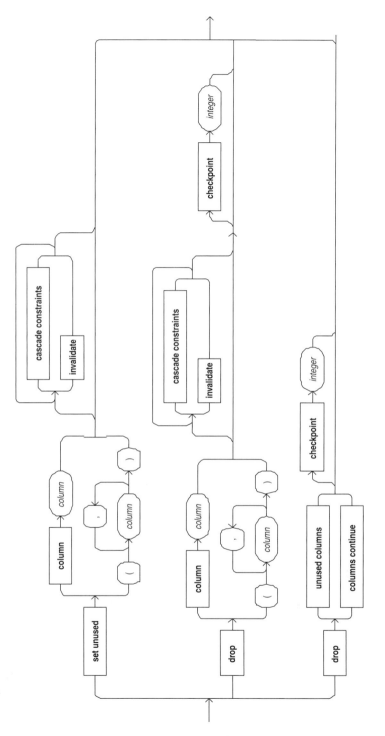

Rename column

Modify collection retrieval

Constraint

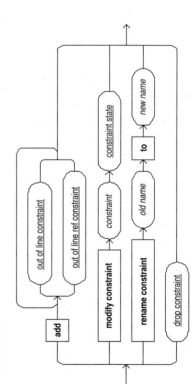

Drop constraint

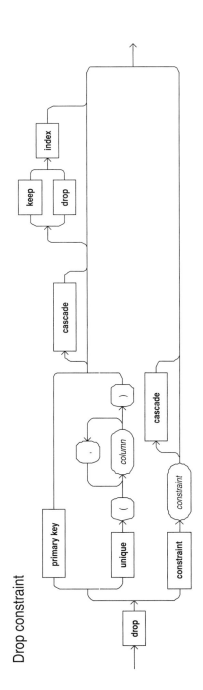

Column properties

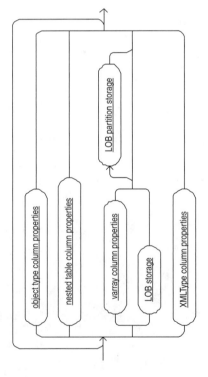

Object type column properties

Substitutable column

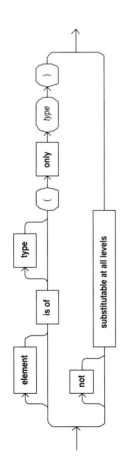

Nested table column properties

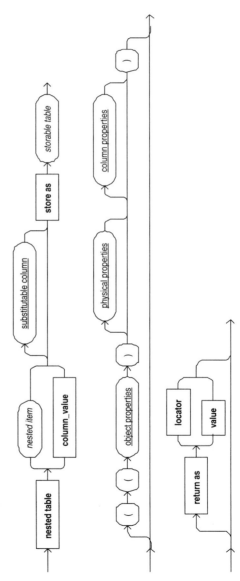

Object properties

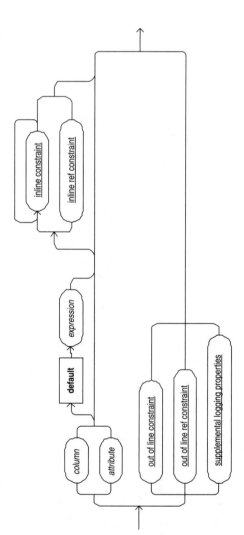

Supplemental logging properties

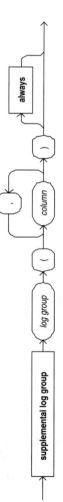

Physical properties

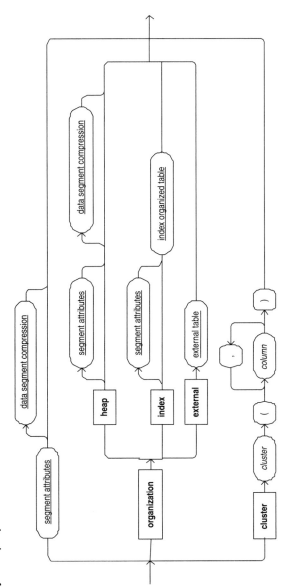

Varray column properties

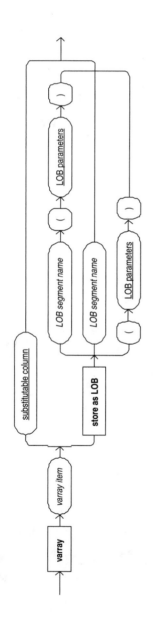

LOB storage

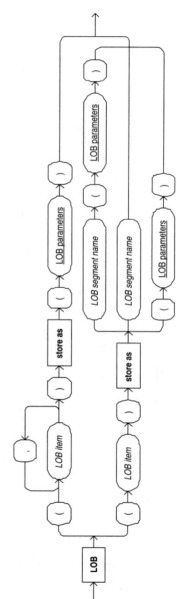

LOB parameters

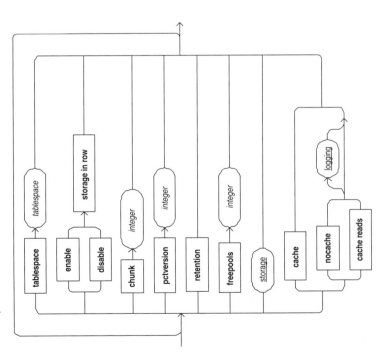

Modify LOB storage

Modify LOB parameters

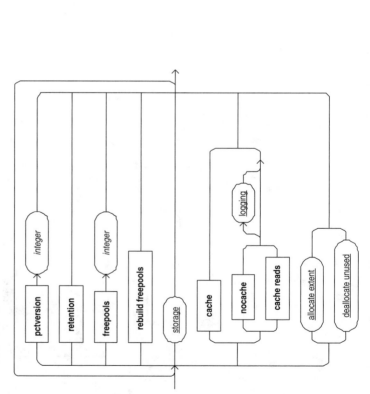

Alter varray column properties

LOB partition storage

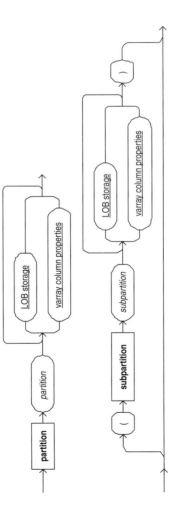

XMLType column properties

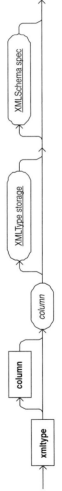

XMLType storage

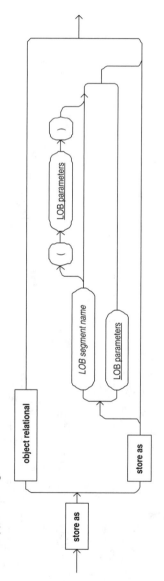

XMLSchema spec

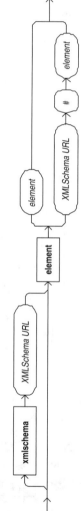

Alter external table

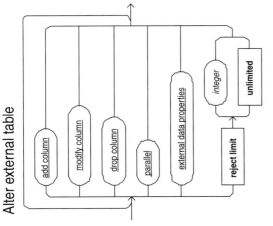

External data properties

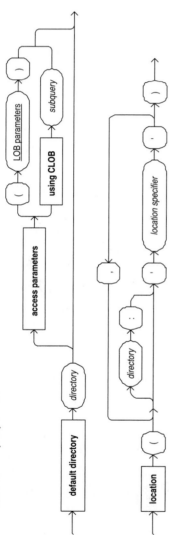

Alter table partitioning

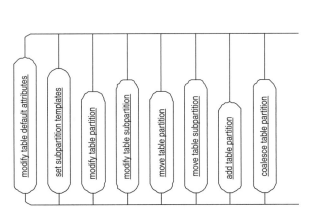

- modify table default attributes
- set subpartition templates
- modify table partition
- modify table subpartition
- move table partition
- move table subpartition
- add table partition
- coalesce table partition

Alter table partitioning (cont.)

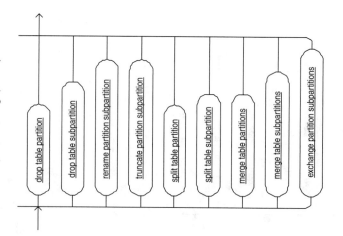

Modify table default attributes

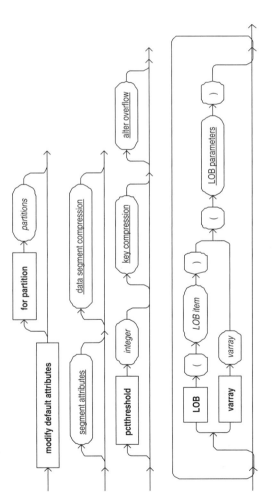

Set subpartition template

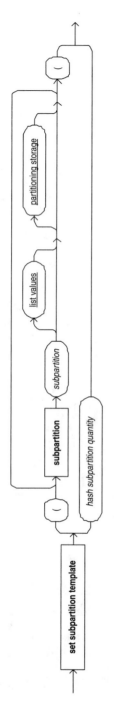

Modify table partition

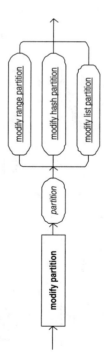

Modify range partition

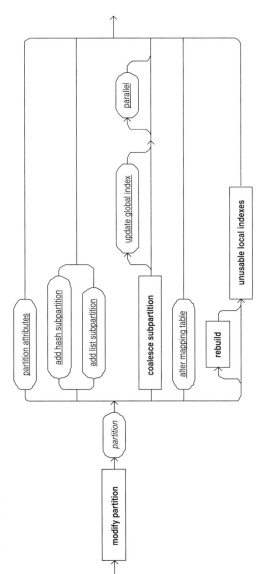

Modify hash partition

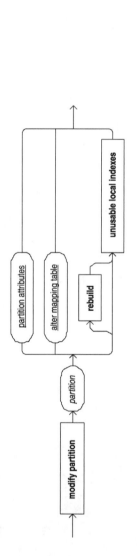

Modify list partition

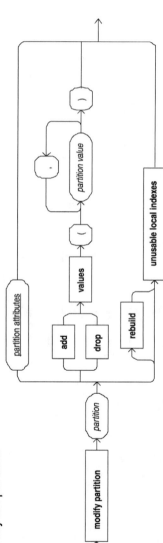

Modify table subpartition

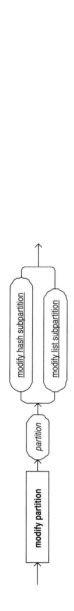

Move table partition

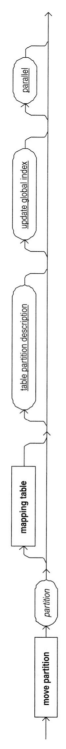

Move table subpartition

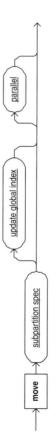

Add table partition

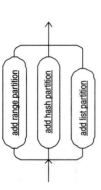

Add range partition

Add hash partition

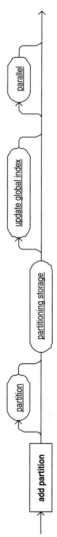

Add list partition

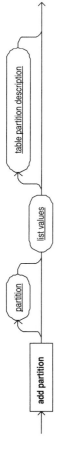

Coalesce table partition

Drop table partition

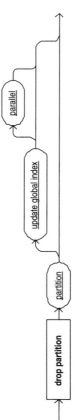

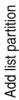

Drop table subpartition

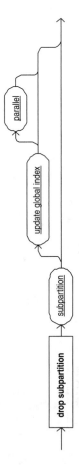

Rename partition subpartition

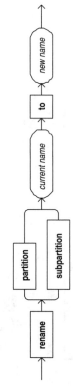

Truncate partition subpartition

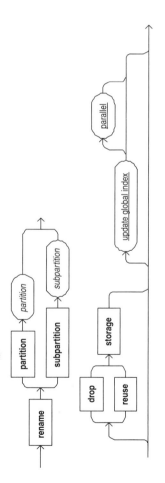

Split table partition

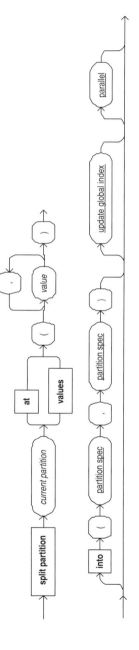

Split table subpartition

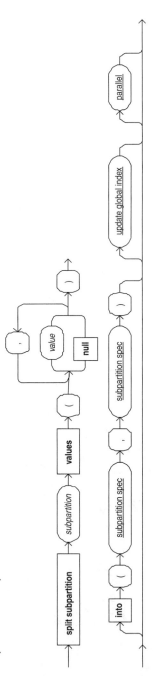

Merge table partitions

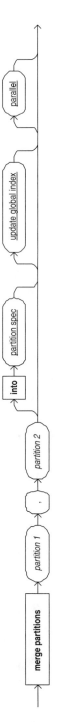

Merge table subpartitions

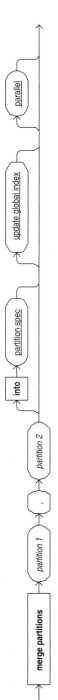

Exchange partition subpartition

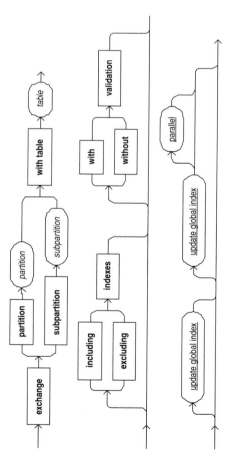

List values

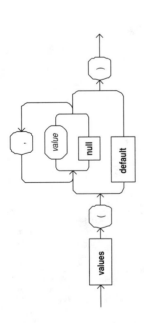

Range values

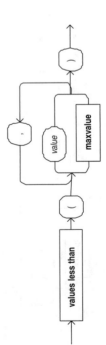

Partitioning storage

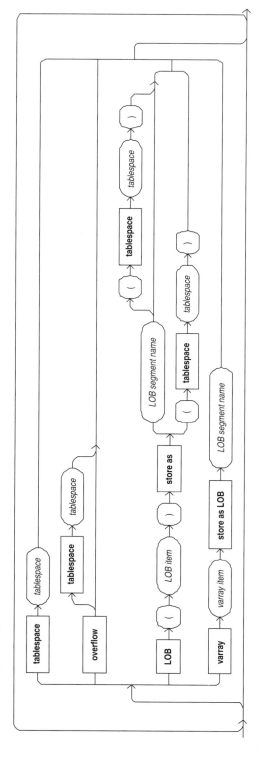

Partition attributes

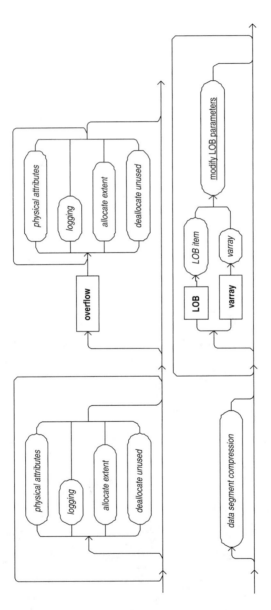

Add hash subpartition

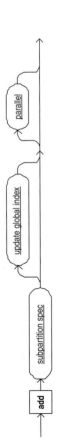

Add list subpartition

Modify hash subpartition

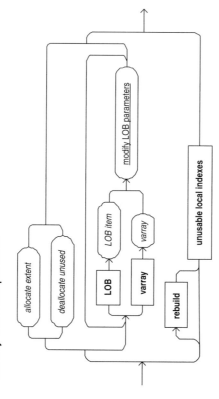

Modify list subpartition

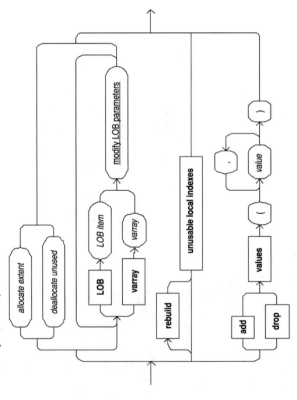

Table partition description

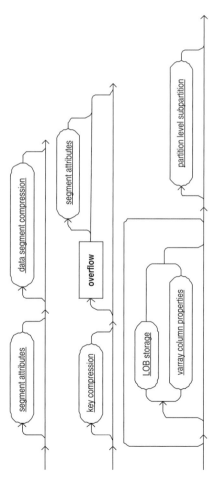

Partition level subpartition

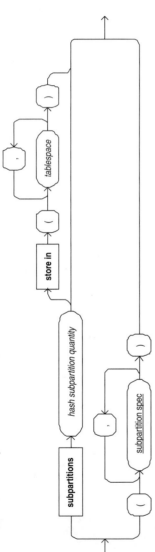

Partition spec

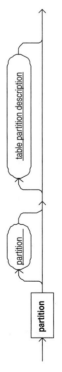

Subpartition spec

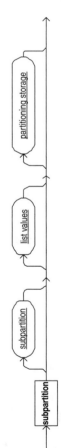

Update global index

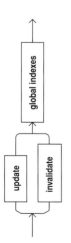

Parallel

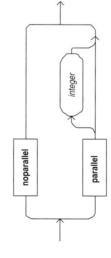

Move table

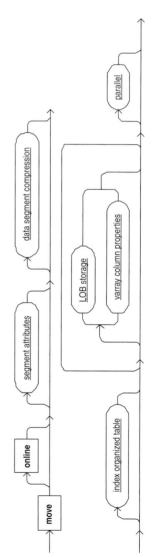

Enable disable

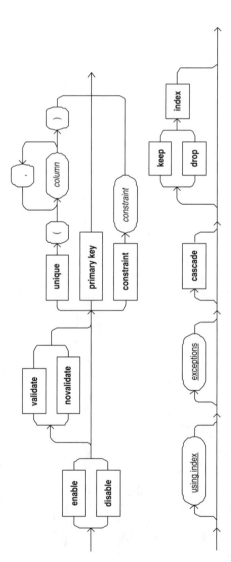

Using index

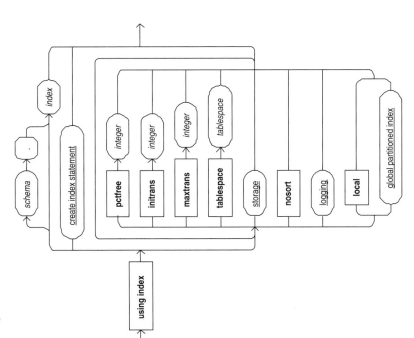

Global partitioned index

Index partitioning

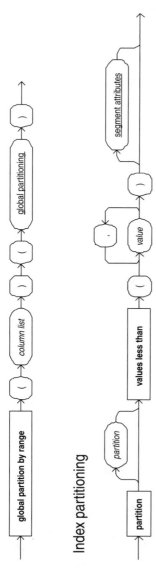

Alter Tablespace

Alter the status and parameters of a tablespace.

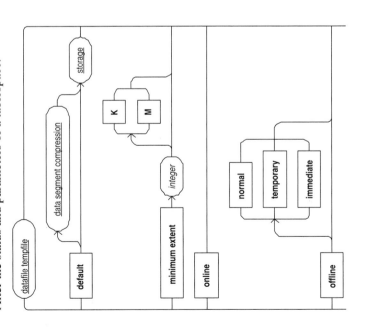

Alter Tablespace (cont.)

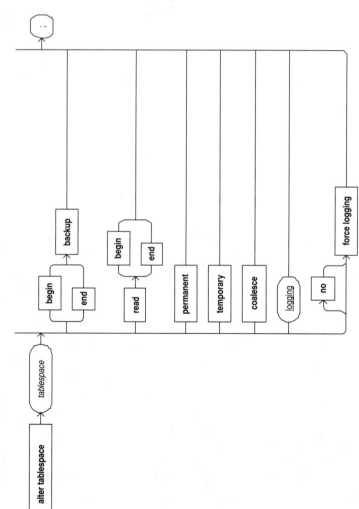

Datafile tempfile

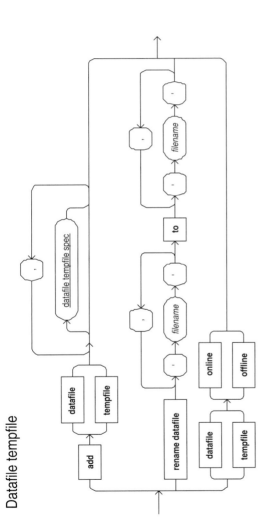

Alter Trigger

Enable, disable, or compile a trigger.

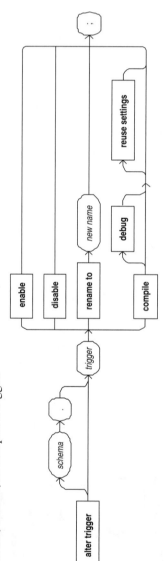

Alter Type

Modify the properties of a Type.

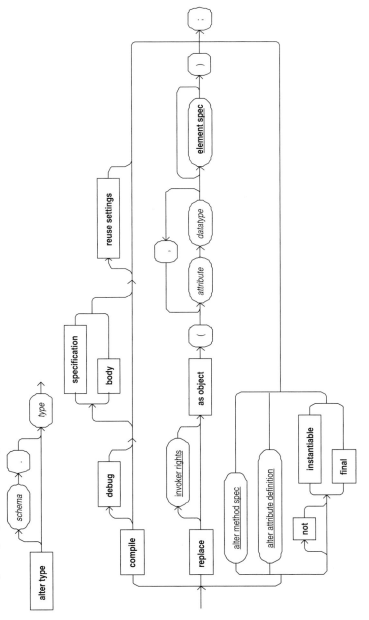

Invoker rights

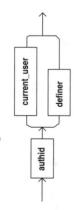

Element spec

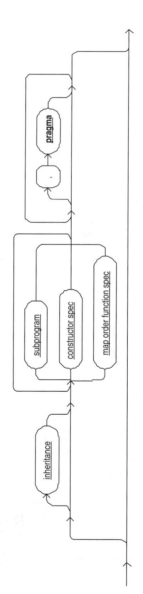

Inheritance

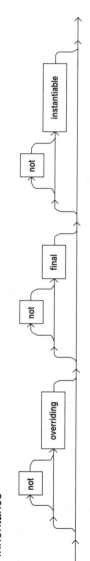

Subprogram

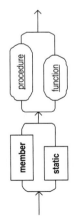

Procedure spec

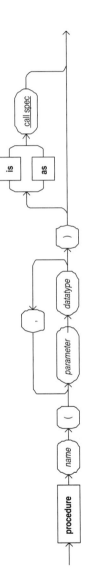

Function spec

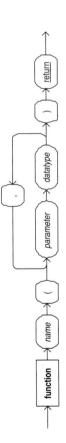

Constructor spec

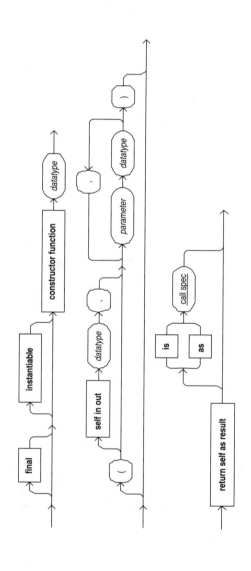

Map order function spec

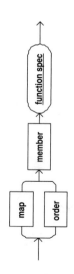

Pragma

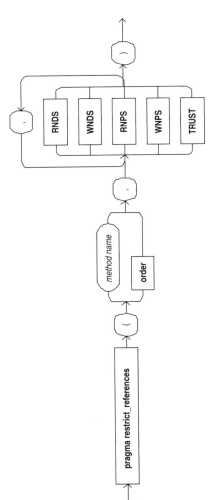

Alter method spec

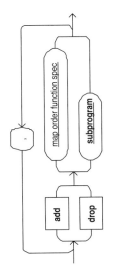

Alter attribute definition

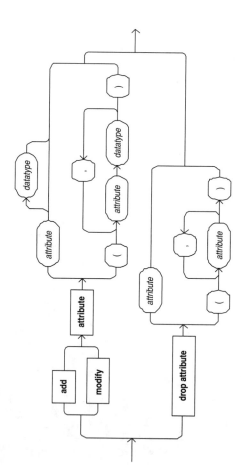

Dependent handling

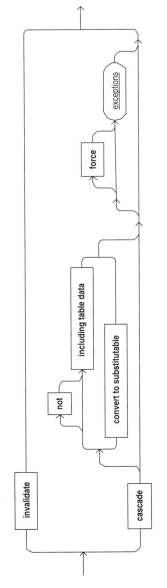

Exceptions

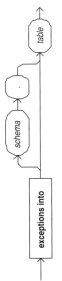

Alter User

Modify the authentication parameters and storage parameters of a user.

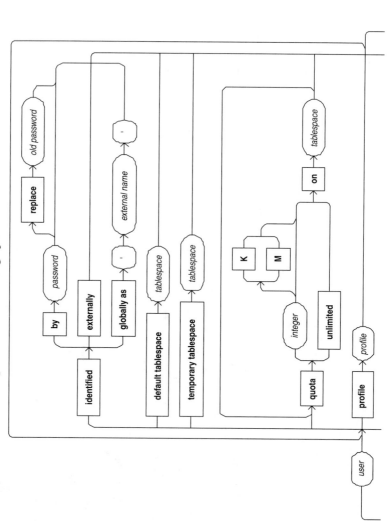

Alter User (cont.)

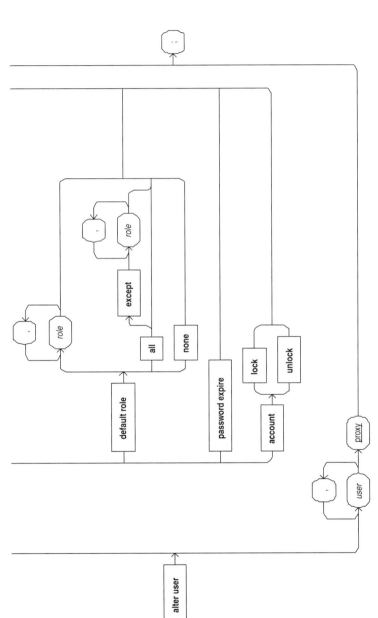

Proxy

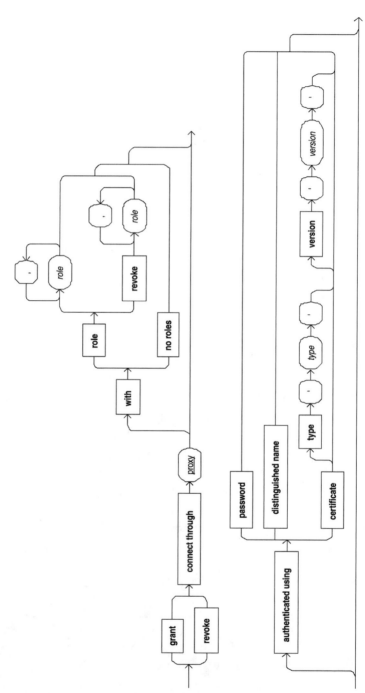

Alter View

Modify the constraints or explicitly recompile a view

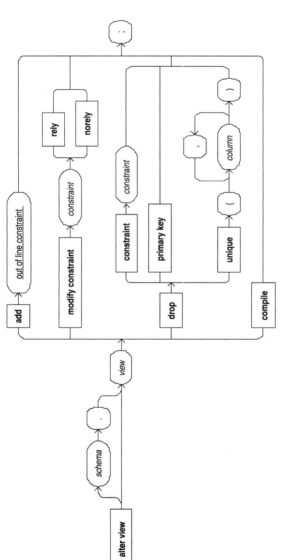

ANALYZE

Collect statistics and validate index structures.

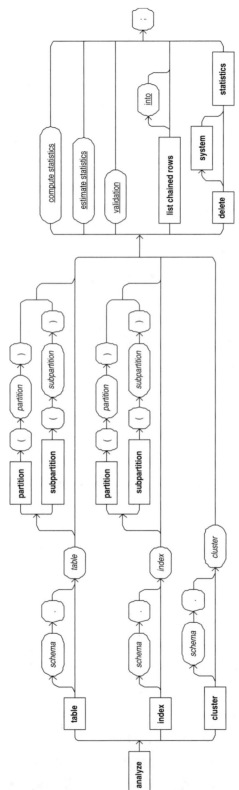

Compute statistics

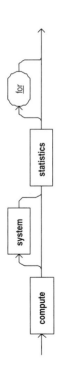

Estimate statistics

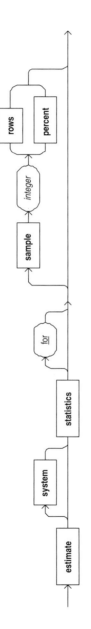

Validation

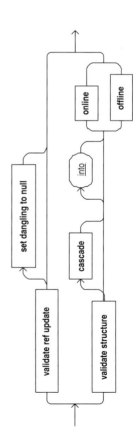

For

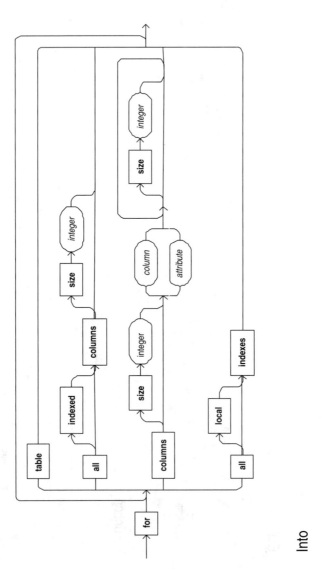

Into

ASSOCIATE STATISTICS

Associate a statistics type with a column, function, package, type, index, or indextype.

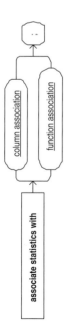

Column association

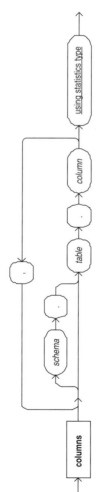

Function association

Using statistics type

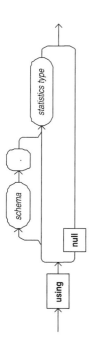

Default cost

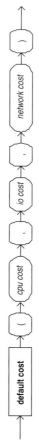

Default selectivity

AUDIT

Enable the auditing of specific schema objects

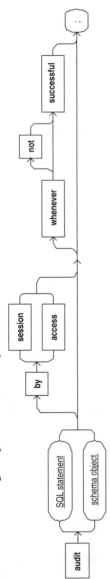

SQL statement

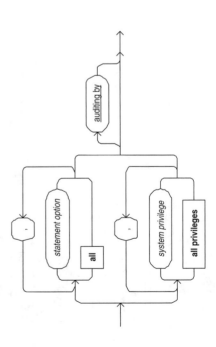

Auditing by

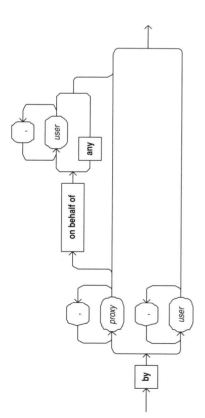

Schema object

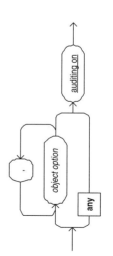

Auditing on

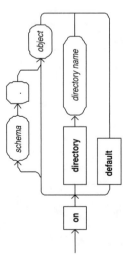

CALL

Execute a routine

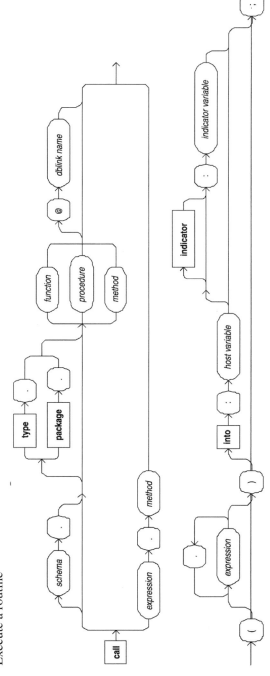

COMMENT

Add a comment to a table, view, materialized view or column.

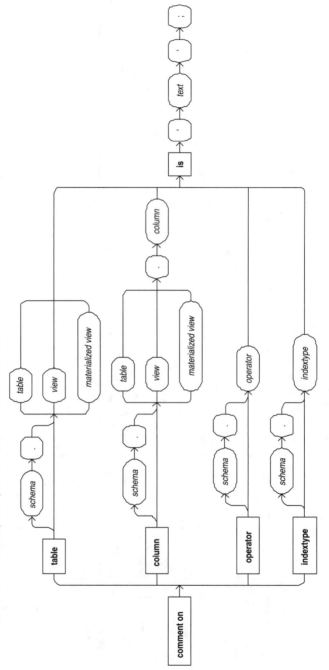

COMMIT

Finish a transaction, making it permanent.

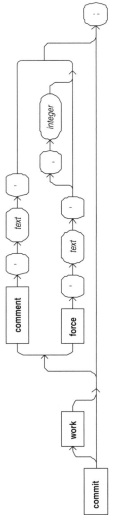

CREATE

Create statements create new objects.

Create Cluster

Create a new cluster in the existing database.

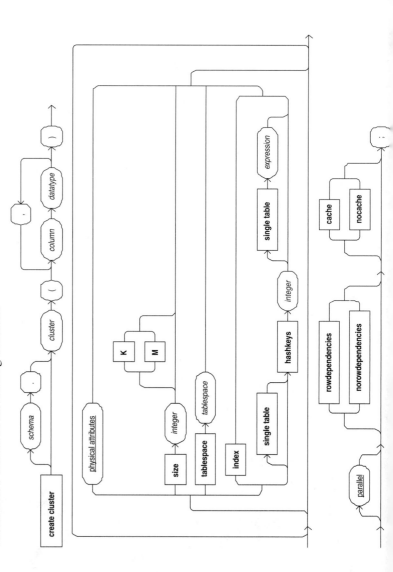

Create Context

Create a context and associate a namespace with external packages.

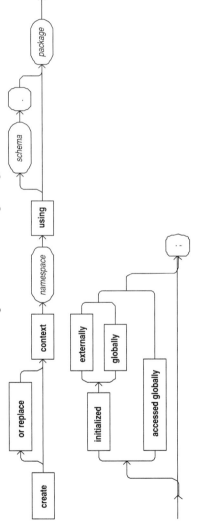

Create Controlfile

Create or recreate a control file.

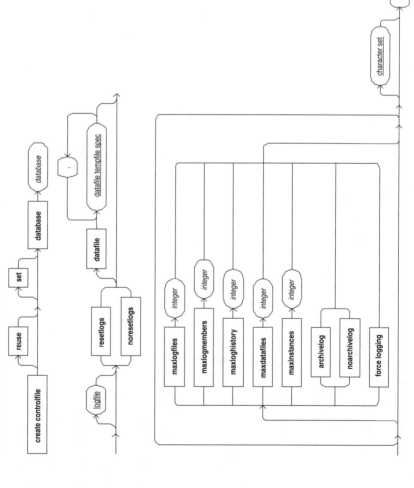

Logfile

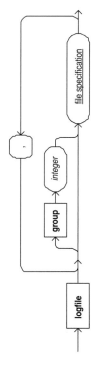

Character set

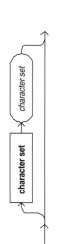

Create Database

Creates a database and erases any data in specified files

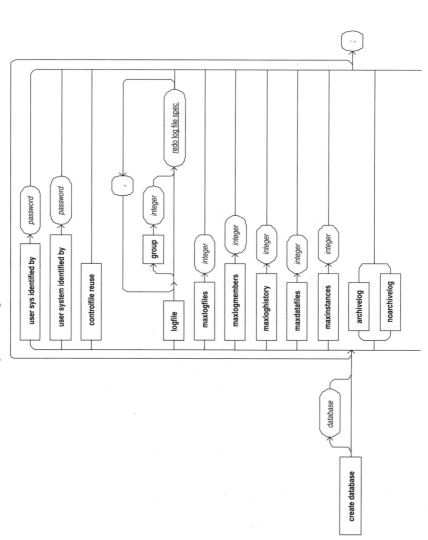

Create database (cont.)

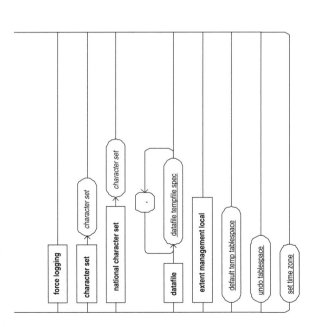

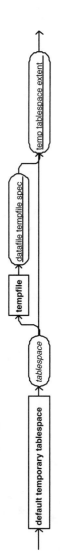

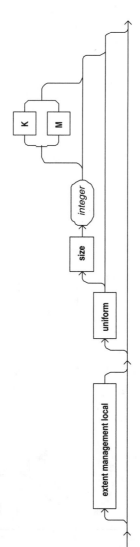

Default temp tablespace

Temp tablespace extent

Undo tablespace

Set time zone

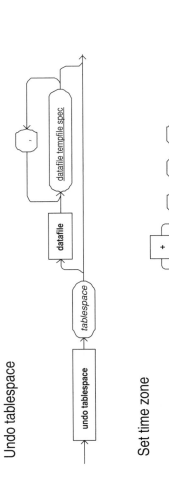

Create Database Link

Create a link to a remote database object.

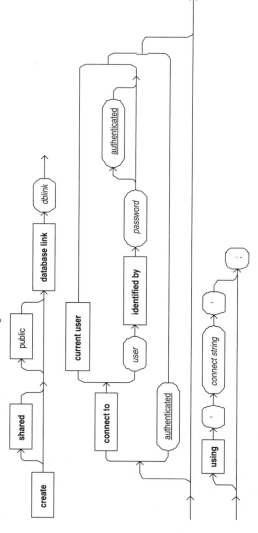

Authenticated

Create Dimension

Create a dimension, a parent child relationship between column set pairs.

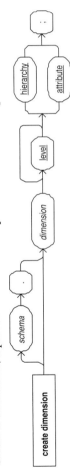

Level

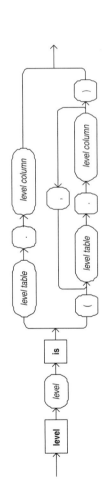

Hierarchy

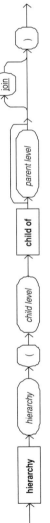

Join

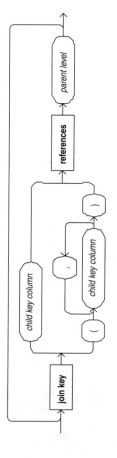

Attribute

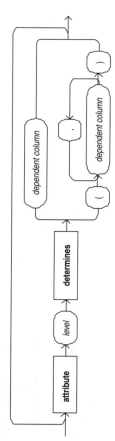

Create Directory

Create a directory.

```
create ─┬─────────────┬─ directory ─( directory )─ as ─( ' )─( path name )─( ' )─( ; )
        └─ or replace ─┘
```

Create Function

Create a standalone stored function or call.

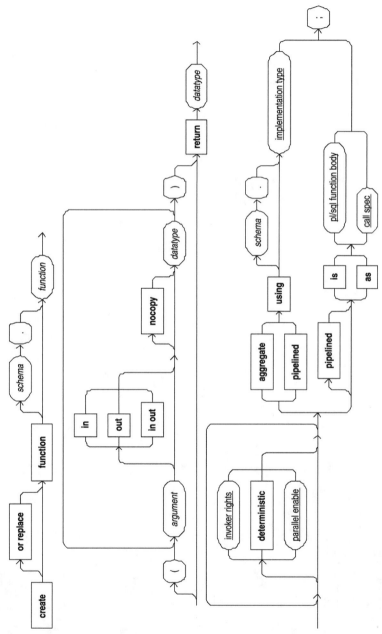

Invoker rights

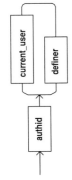

Parallel enable

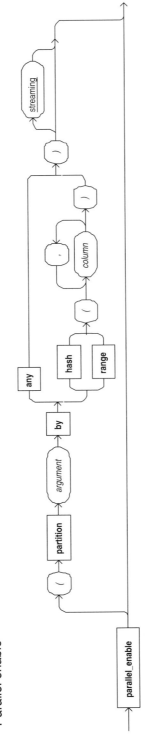

Streaming

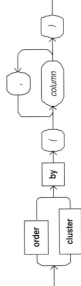

Call spec

Java declaration

C declaration

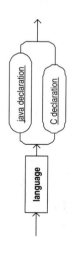
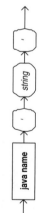
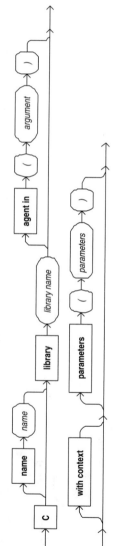

Create Index

Create an index.

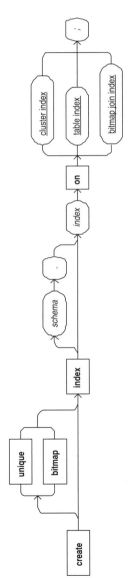

Cluster index

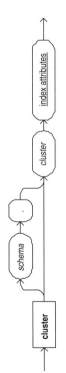

Table index

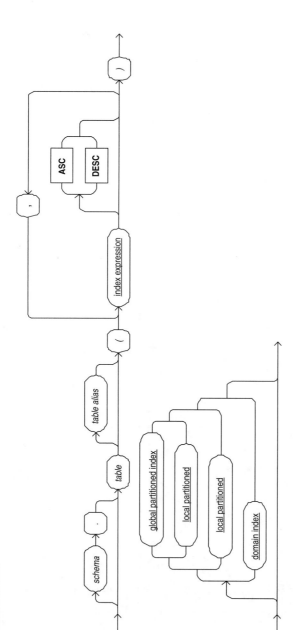

Bitmap join index

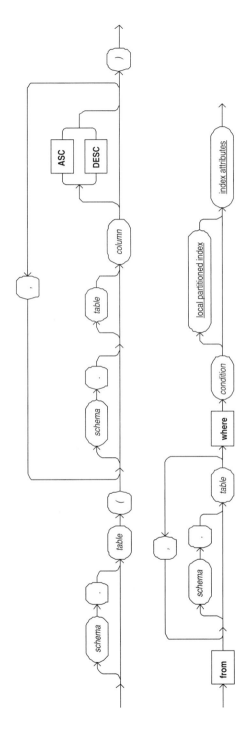

Index expression

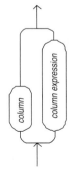

Index attributes

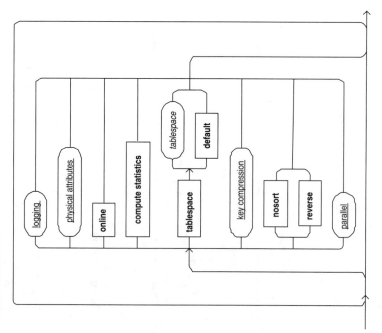

Physical attributes

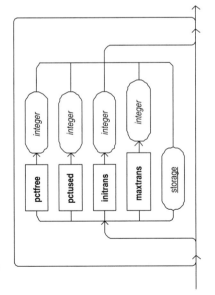

Logging

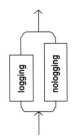

Key compression

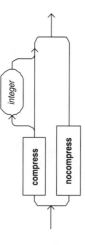

Domain index

Global partitioned index

Global partitioning

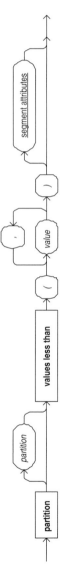

Local partitioned index

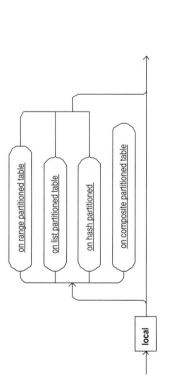

On range partitioned table

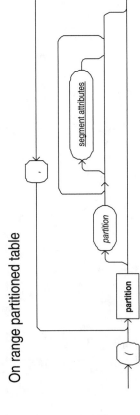

On list partitioned table

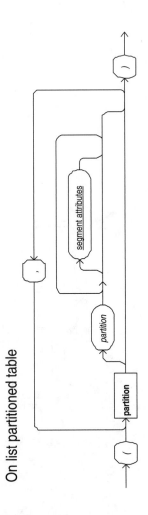

Segment attributes

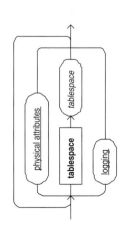

On hash partitioned table

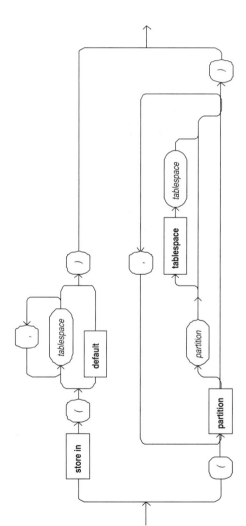

On composite partitioned table

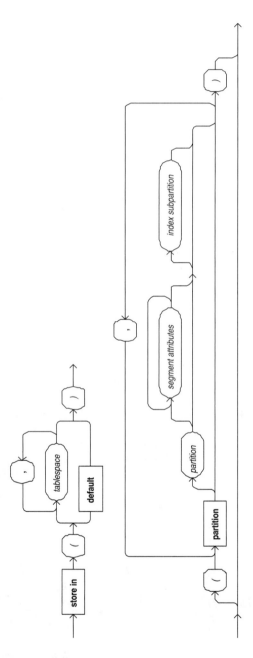

Index subpartition

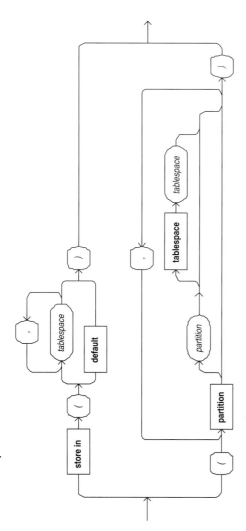

Parallel

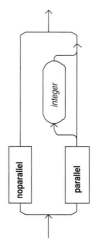

Create Indextype

Create an indextype object.

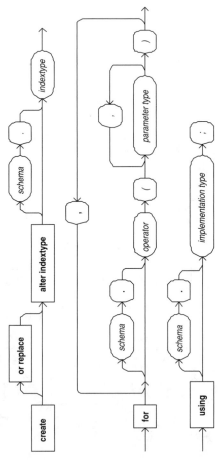

Create Java

Create a Java object containing a Java resource, class or source.

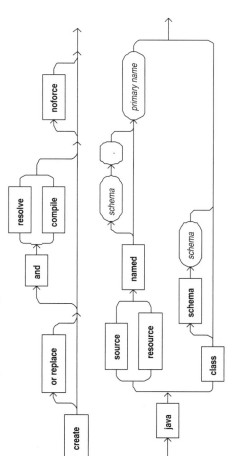

Create Java (cont.)

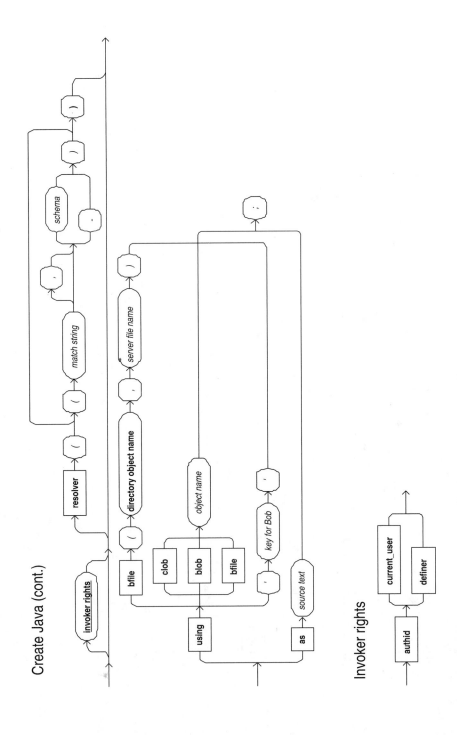

Invoker rights

Create Library

Create a callable object associated with an OS shared library.

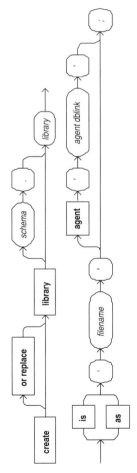

Create Materialized View

Create a materialized view of the results of a query.

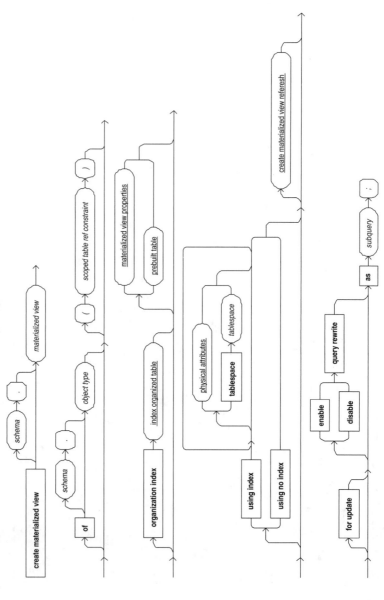

Materialized view properties

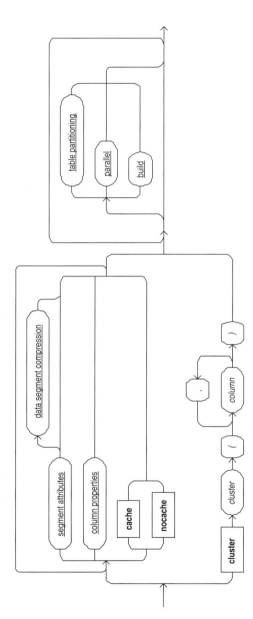

Prebuilt table

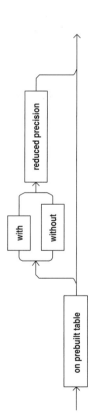

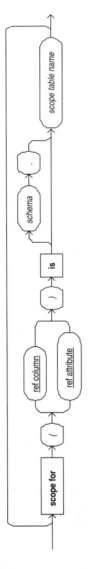

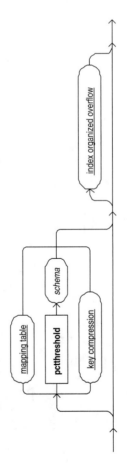

Scoped table ref constraint

Index organized table

Key compression

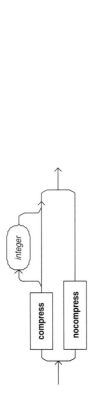

Index organized overflow

Create materialized view refresh

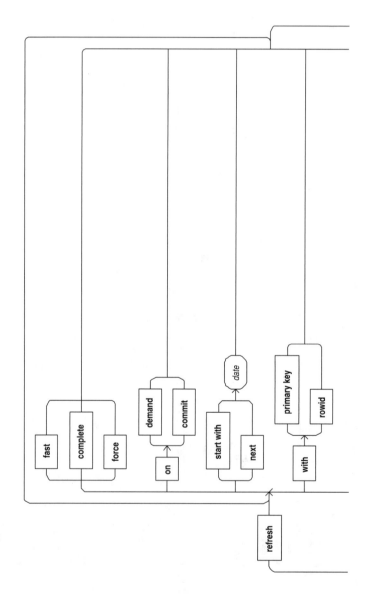

Create materialized view refresh (cont.)

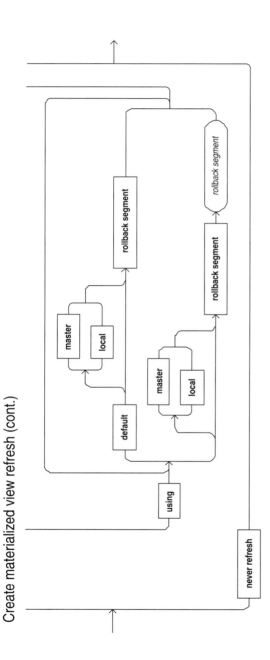

Segment attributes

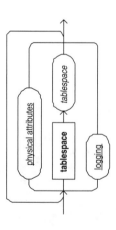

Physical attributes

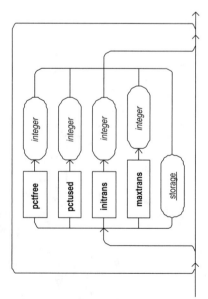

Logging

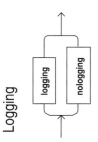

Data segment compression

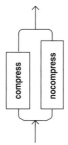

Physical attributes

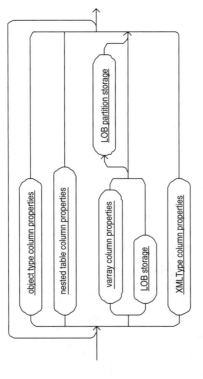

Object type column properties

Substitutable column

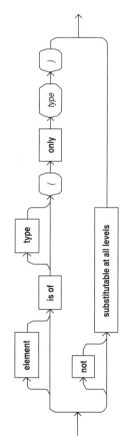

Nested table column properties

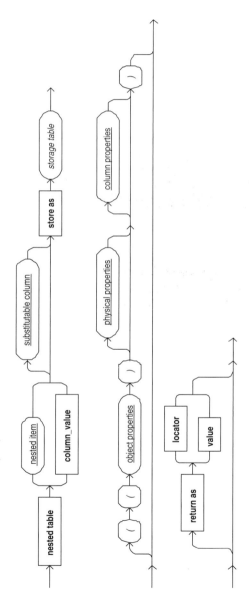

Varray column properties

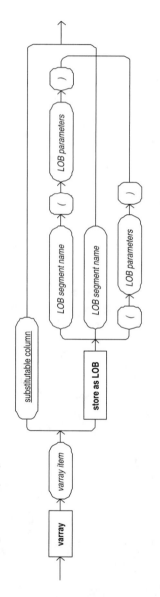

LOB storage

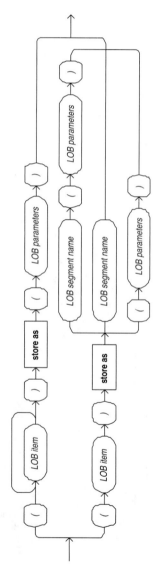

LOB parameters

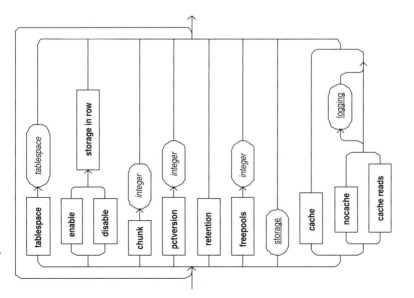

LOB partition storage

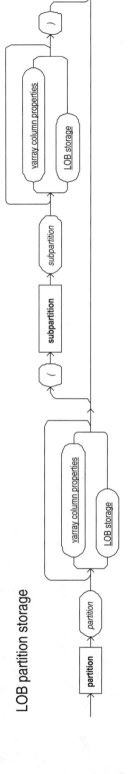

Parallel

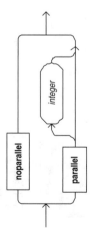

Build

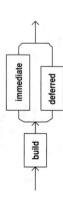

Create Materialized View Log

Create a materialized view log.

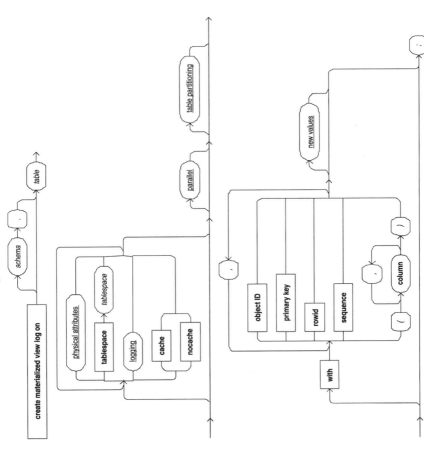

New values

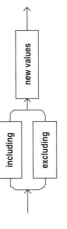

Create Operator

Create an operator and define its bindings.

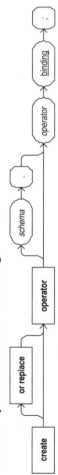

Binding

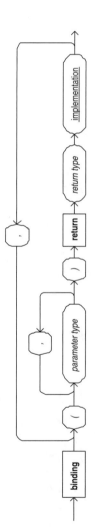

Implementation

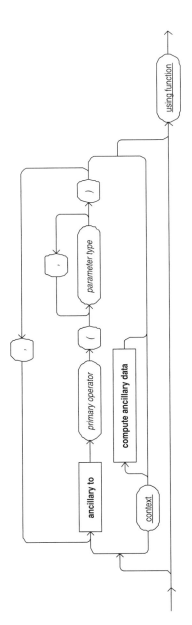

Context

Using function

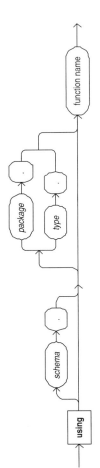

Create Outline

Create an outline for the optimizer.

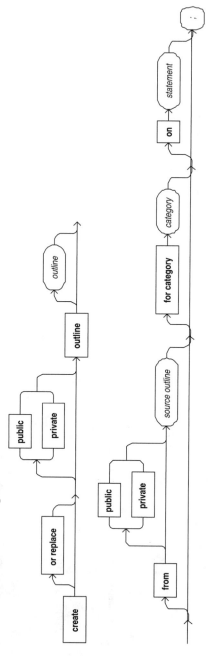

Create Package

Create a package of stored procedures, functions and other objects.

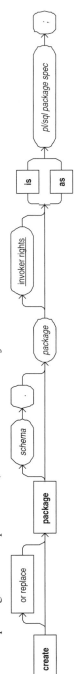

Invoker rights

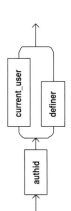

Create Package Body

Create the body of a stored package.

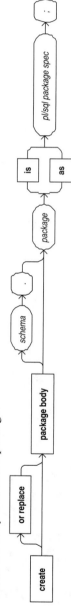

Create pfile

Export a binary parameter file into a text initialization file.

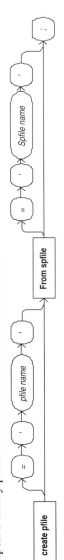

Create Procedure

Create a standalone stored procedure.

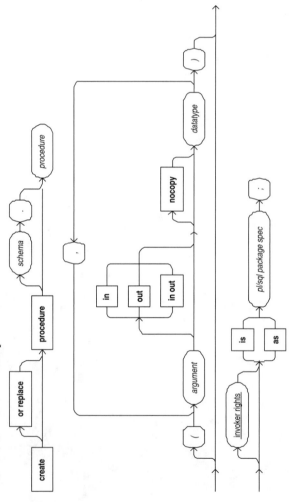

Invoker rights

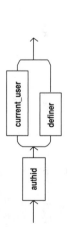

Call spec

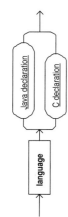

Java declaration

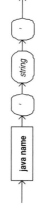

C declaration

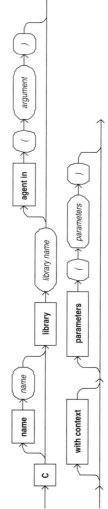

Create Profile

Create a profile to set limits on database resources.

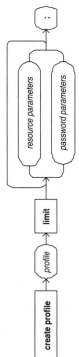

Resource parameters

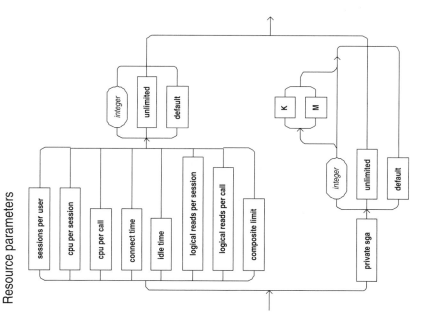

Resource parameters

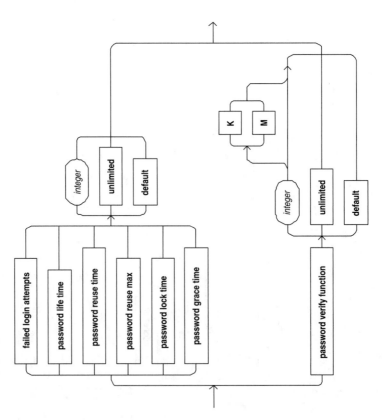

Create Role

Create a role – a grouping of a privileges that can be granted to users or other roles.

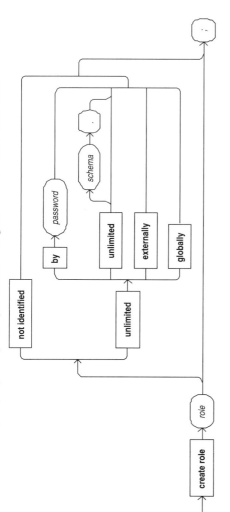

Create Rollback Segment

Create a rollback segment.

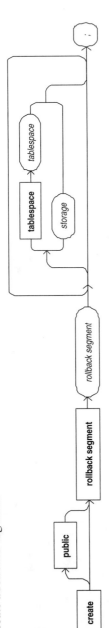

Create Schema

Create a multiple tables, views and grants as a single transaction.

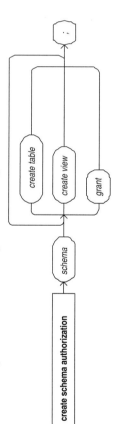

Create Sequence
Create a sequence.

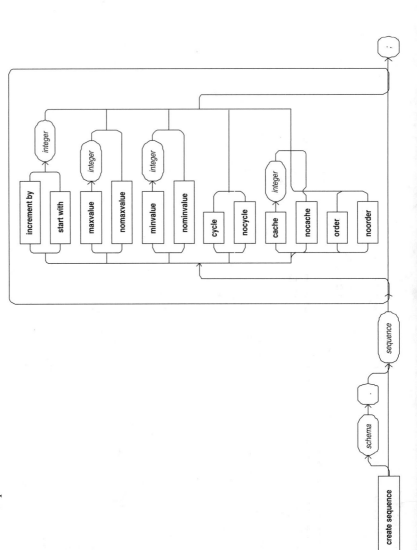

Create spfile

Create a binary server parameter file from a client initialization file.

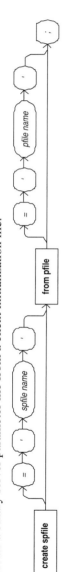

Create Synonym

Create a synonym to a database object.

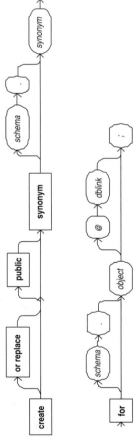

Create Table

Create a table.

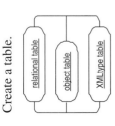

Relational table

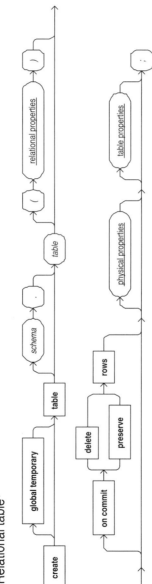

Object table

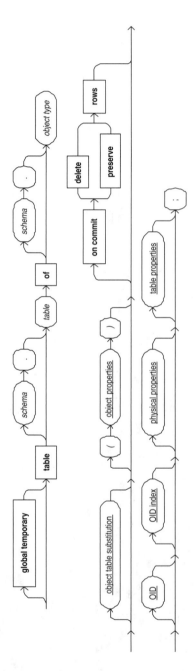

XMLType table

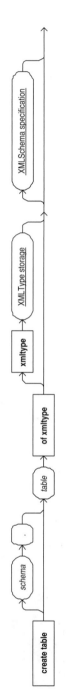

Relational properties

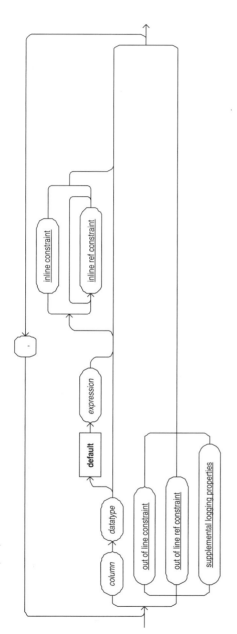

Object table substitution

Object properties

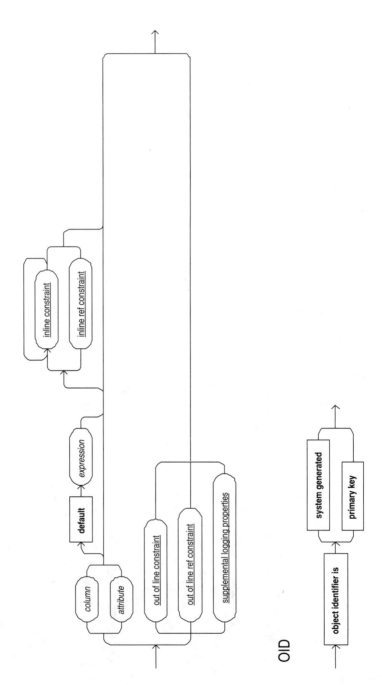

OID

OID index

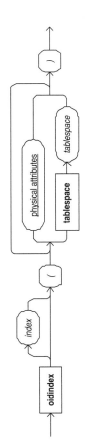

Physical properties

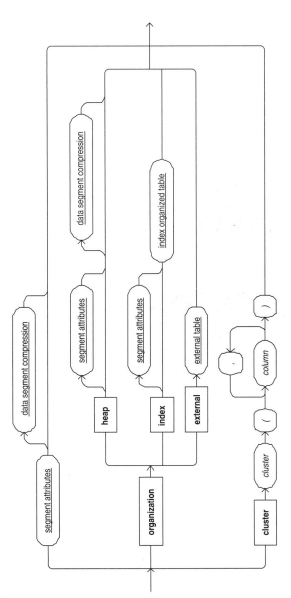

Segment attributes

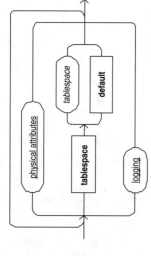

Physical attributes

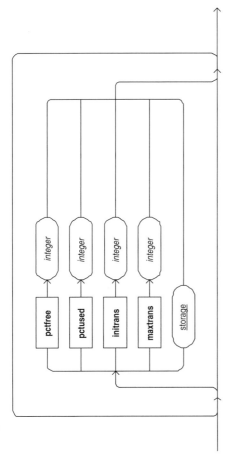

Data segment compression

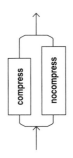

Table properties

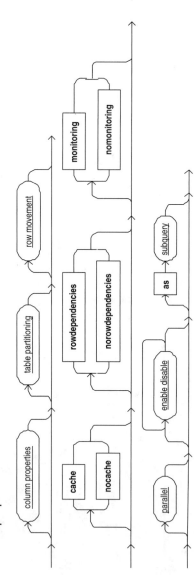

Column properties

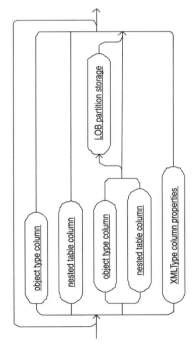

Object type column properties

Substitutable column

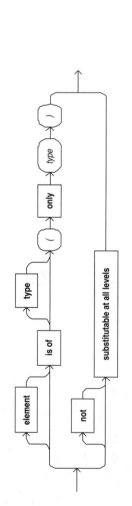

Nested table column properties

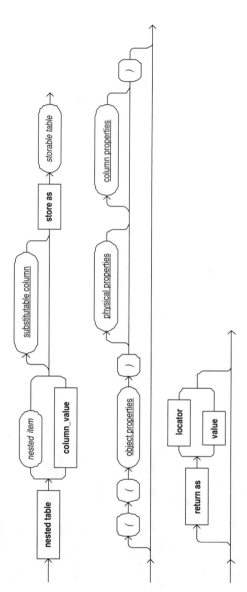

Varray column properties

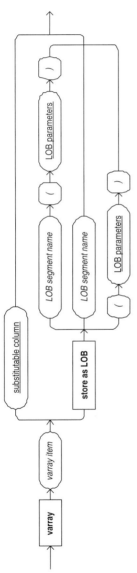

LOB storage

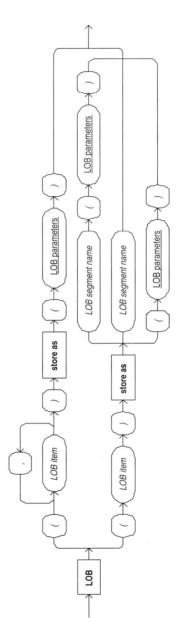

LOB parameters

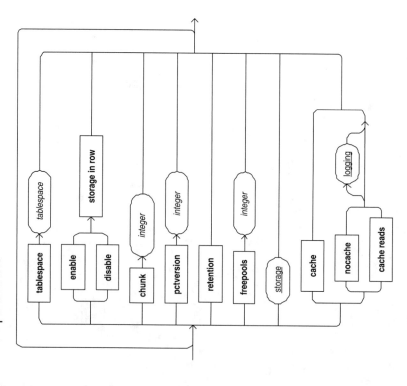

Logging

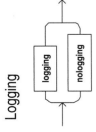

LOB partition storage

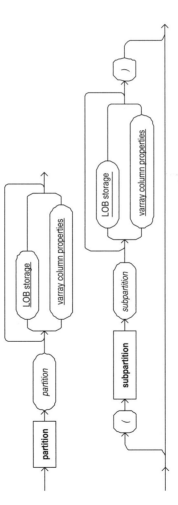

XMLType column properties

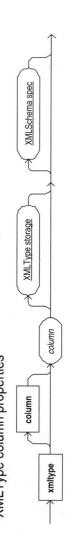

XMLType storage

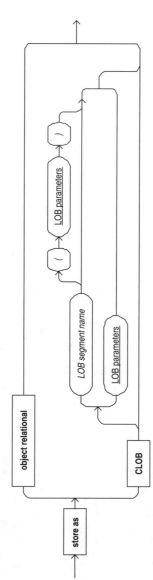

XMLSchema spec

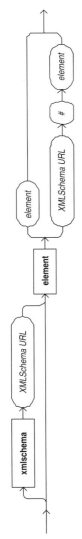

Row movement

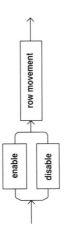

Index organized table

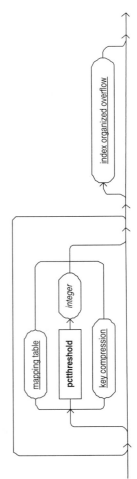

Mapping table

Key compression

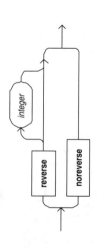

Index organized overflow

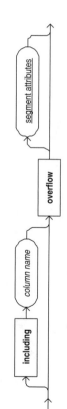

Supplemental logging properties

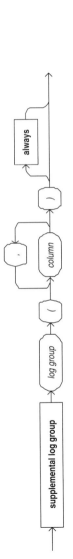

External table

External data properties

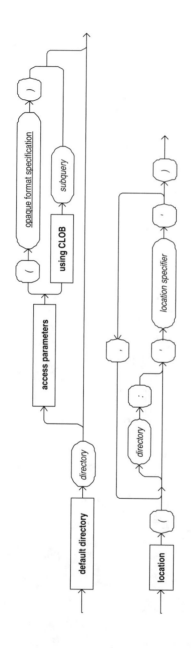

Table partitioning

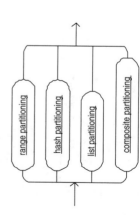

Range partitioning

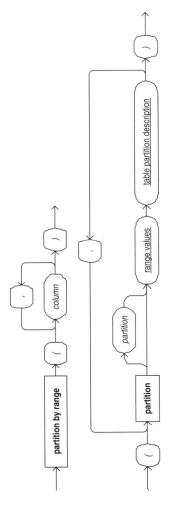

Hash partitioning

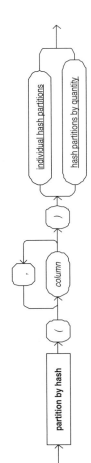

List partitioning

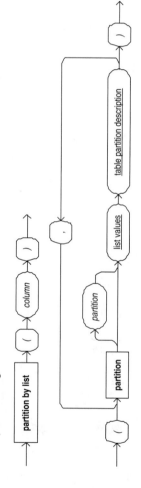

Composite partitioning

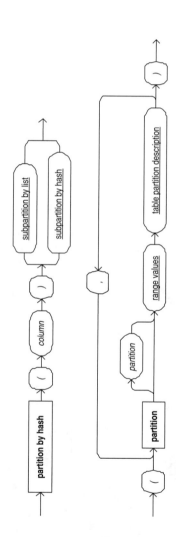

Subpartition by hash

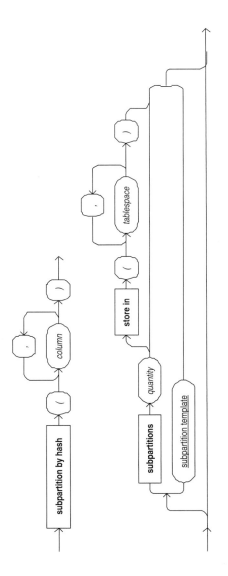

Individual hash partitions

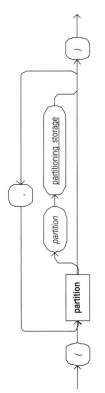

Hash partitions by quantity

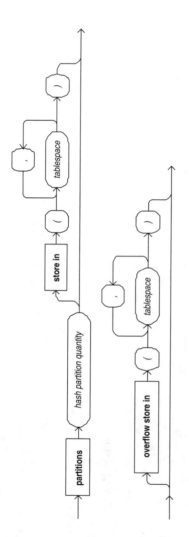

Subpartition by list

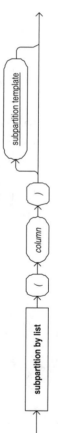

Subpartition template

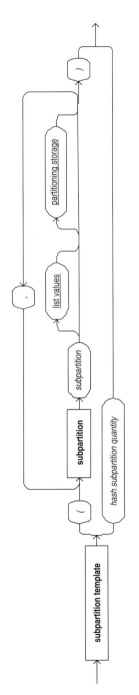

List values

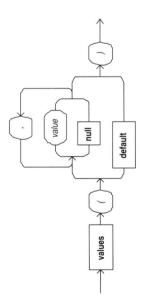

Range values

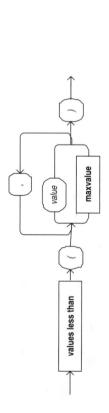

Table partition description

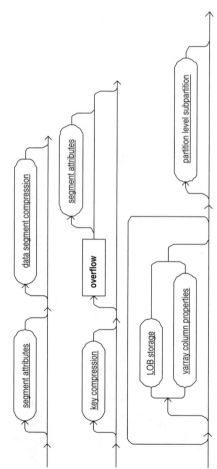

Partition level subpartition

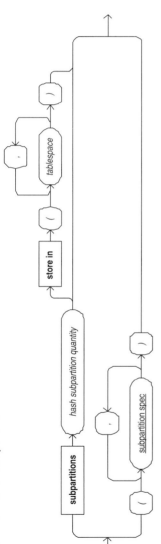

Subpartition spec

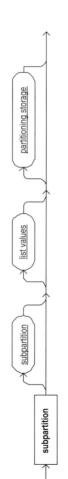

Partitioning storage

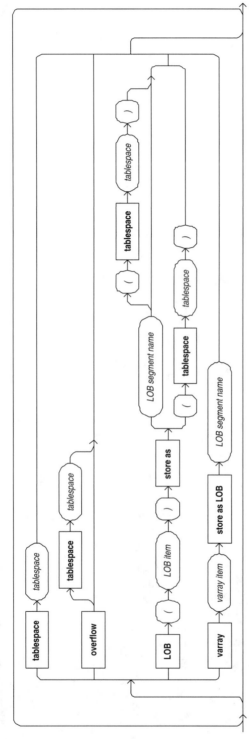

Parallel

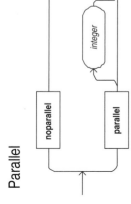

Enable disable

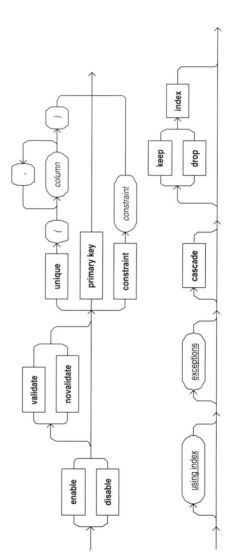

Using index

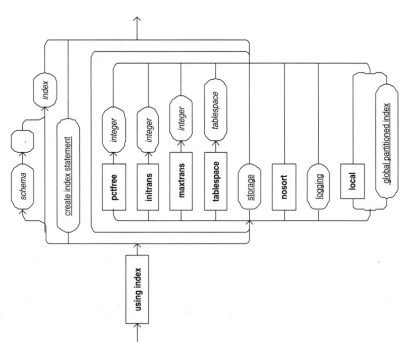

Global partitioned index

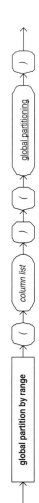

Global partitioning

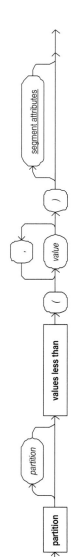

Create Tablespace
Create a new tablespace.

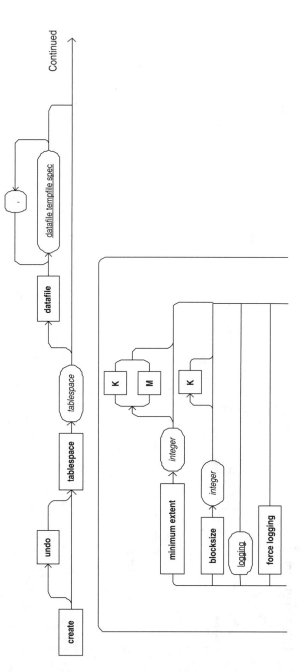

Create Tablespace (cont.)

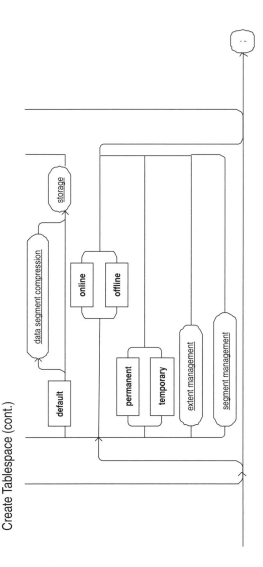

Data segment compression

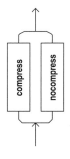

Extent management

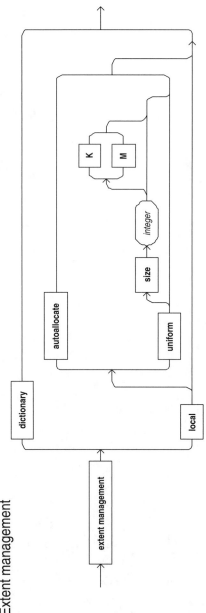

Segment management

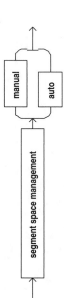

Create Temporary Tablespace

Create a new temporary tablespace.

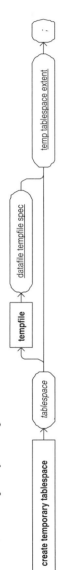

Temp tablespace extent

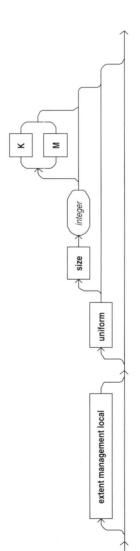

Create Trigger

Create and enable a database trigger.

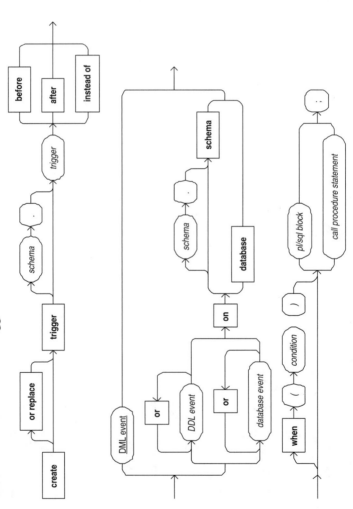

DML event

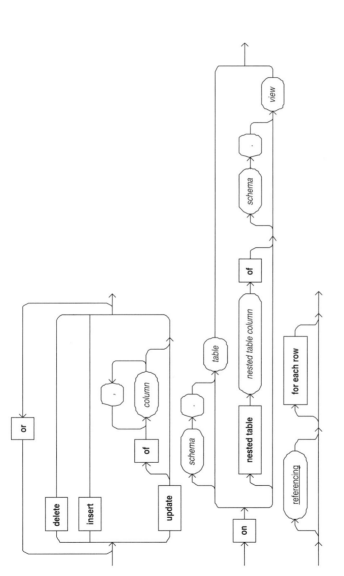

Referencing

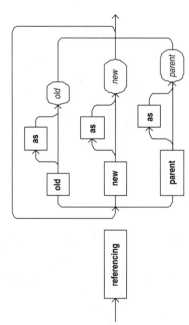

Create Type

Create the specifications for an object type. Use the CREATE TYPE BODY statement to actually assign the code for the type.

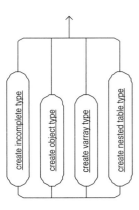

Create incomplete type

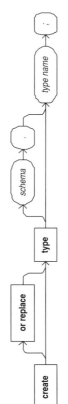

Create object type

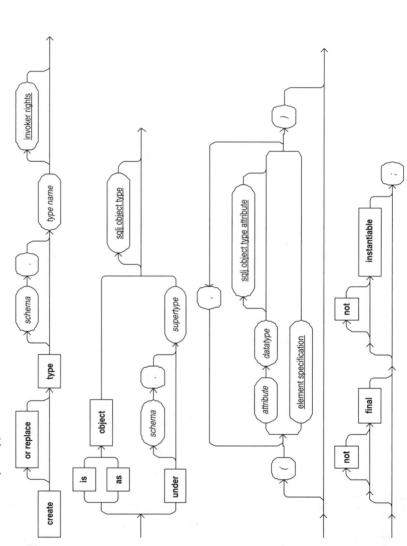

Invoker rights

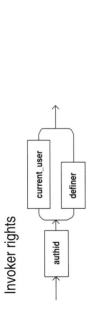

sqlj object type

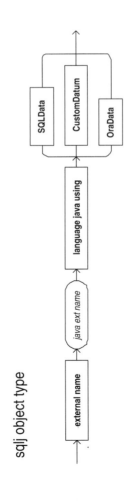

sqlj object type attribute

Element specification

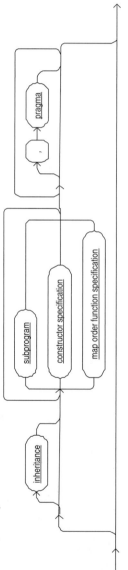

Inheritance

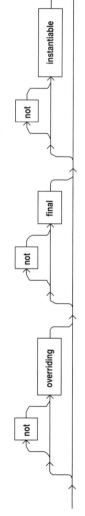

Subprogram

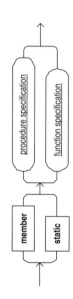

Procedure specification

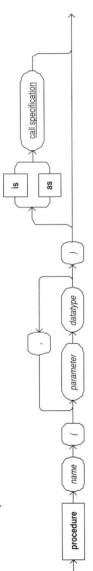

Function specification

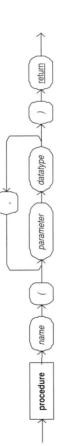

Constructor specification

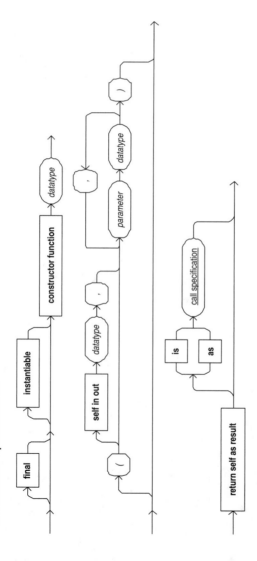

Map order function spec

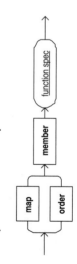

Return

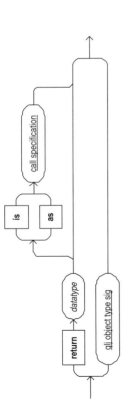

sqlj object type sig

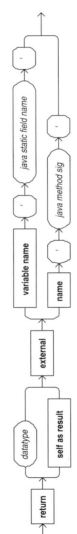

Pragma

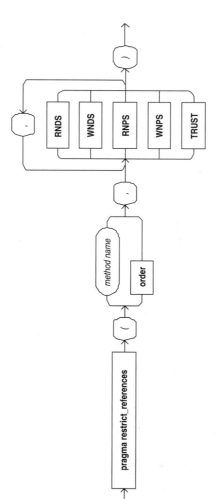

Call specification

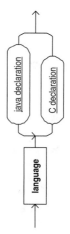

Java declaration

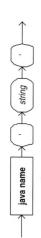

C declaration

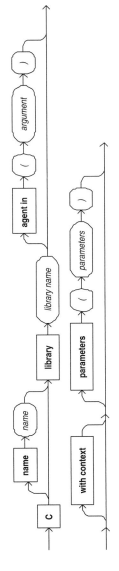

Create varray type

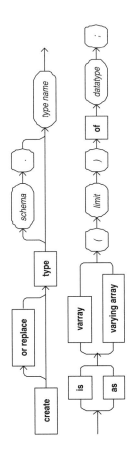

Create nexted table type

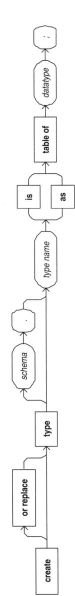

Create Type Body

Create the code for the methods defined by the CREATE TYPE statement.

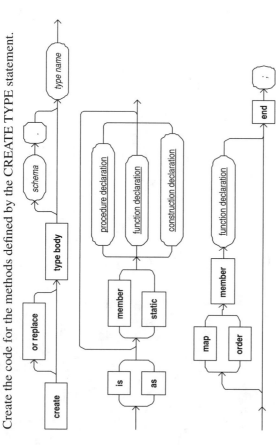

Procedure declaration

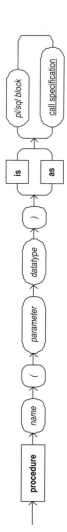

Function declaration

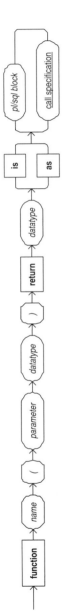

Constructor declaration

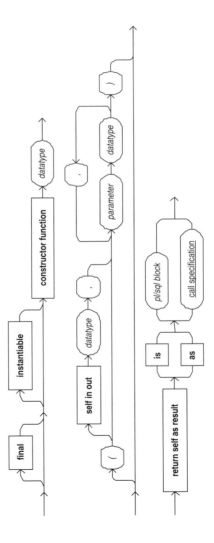

Call specification

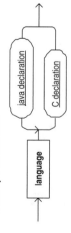

Java declaration

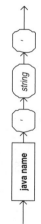

C declaration

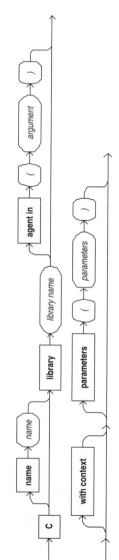

Create User

Create a new user and define storage, password, quotas and other details for the user.

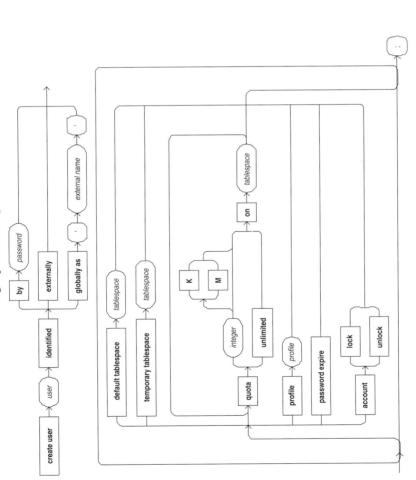

Create View

Define a logical table or *view* of one or more tables or views.

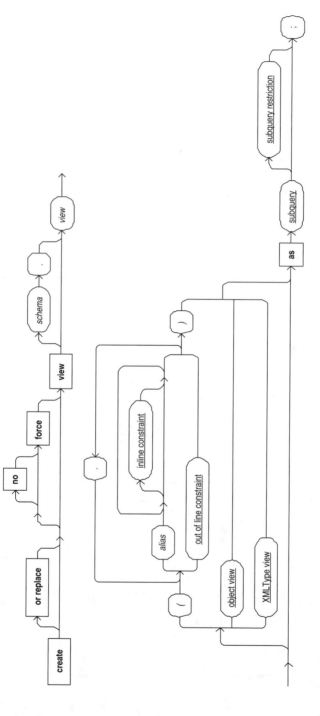

Object view

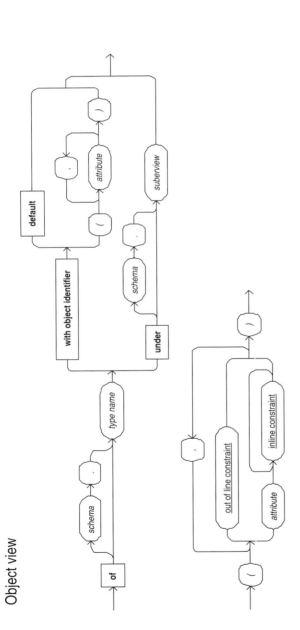

XMLType view

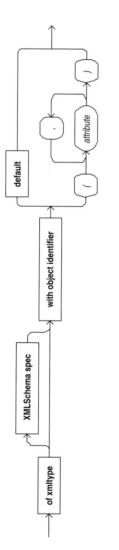

XMLSchema spec

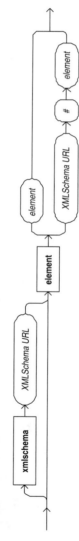

Subquery restriction

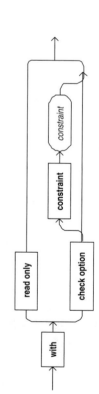

DELETE

Remove rows from a table.

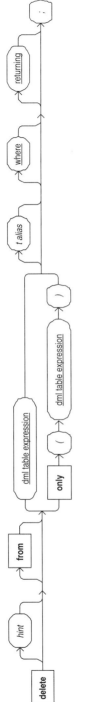

DML table expression

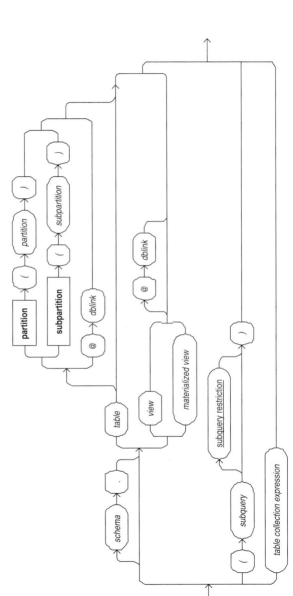

Subquery restriction

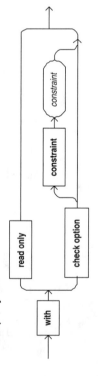

Table collection expression

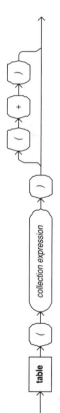

Where

Returning

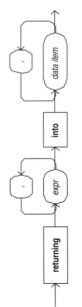

DISASSOCIATE STATISTICS

Disassociate statistics from a column, function, package, type or index.

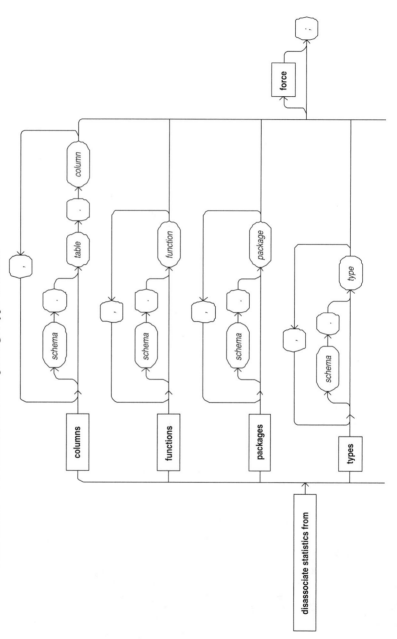

Disassociate Statistics (cont.)

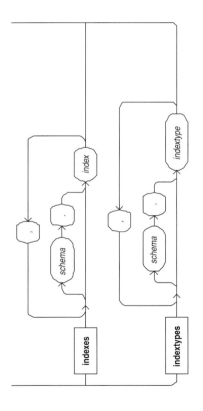

DROP

Drop statements are used to remove objects from the database. You can drop the following objects:

Drop cluster

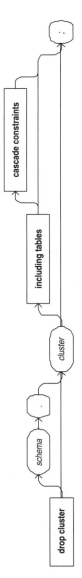

Drop context

Drop database link

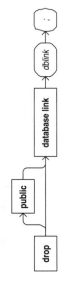

Drop dimension

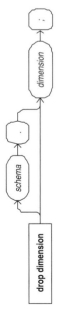

Drop directory

Drop function

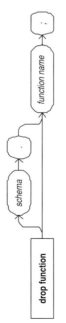

Drop index

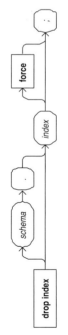

Drop indextype

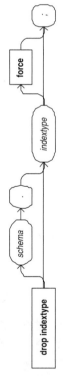

Drop Java

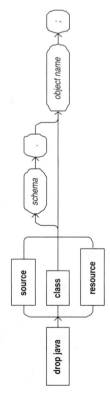

Drop library

Drop materialized view

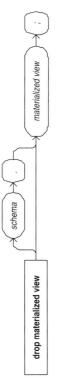

Drop materialized view log

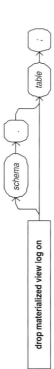

Drop operator

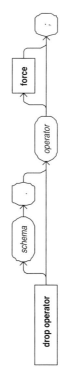

Drop outline

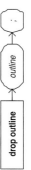

Drop package

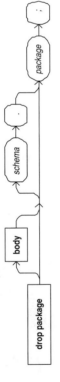

Drop procedure

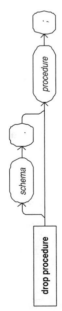

Drop profile

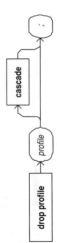

Drop role

Drop rollback segment

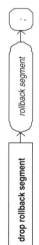

Drop sequence

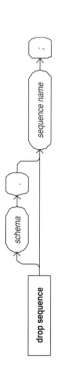

Drop synonym

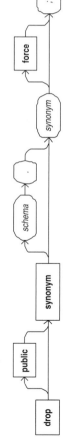

Drop table

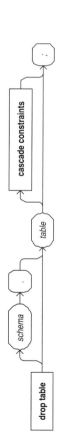

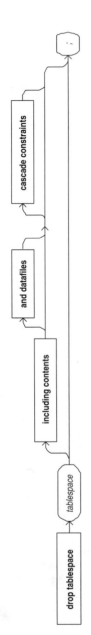

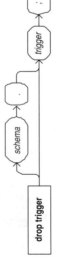

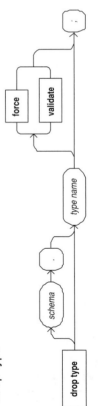

Drop tablespace

Drop trigger

Drop type

Drop type body

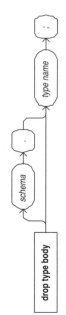

Drop user

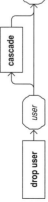

Drop view

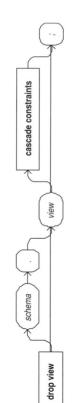

EXPLAIN PLAN

Inserts a row into the specified table describing each step in the SQL statement.

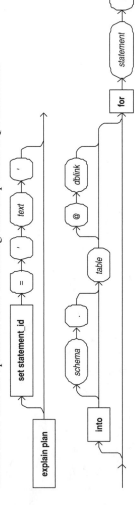

GRANT

Grants system and object privileges, and roles, to users and roles.

Relational table

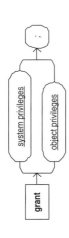

System privileges

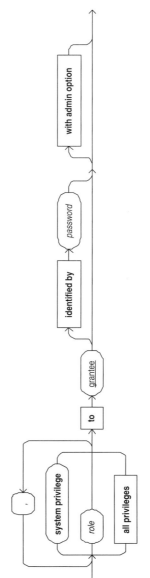

Object privileges

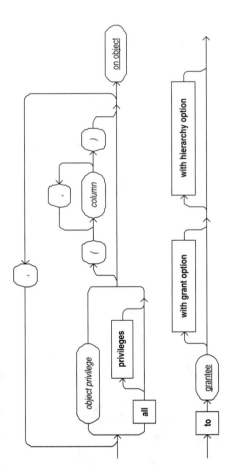

On object

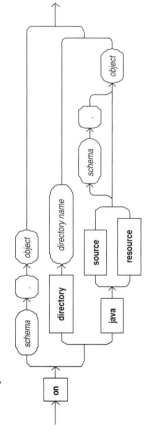

Grantee

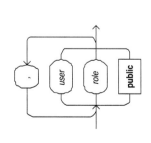

INSERT

Add rows to the database.

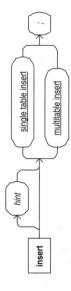

Single table insert

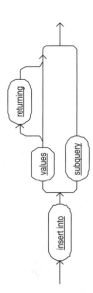

Insert into

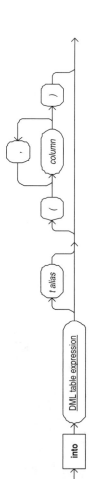

Values

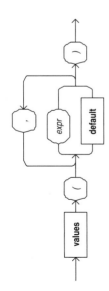

Returning

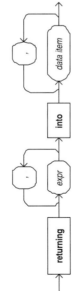

Multitable insert

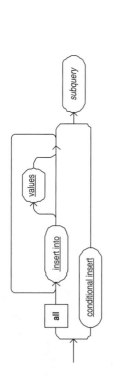

Conditional insert

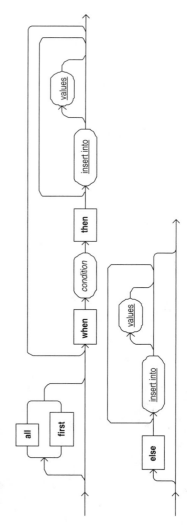

DML table expression

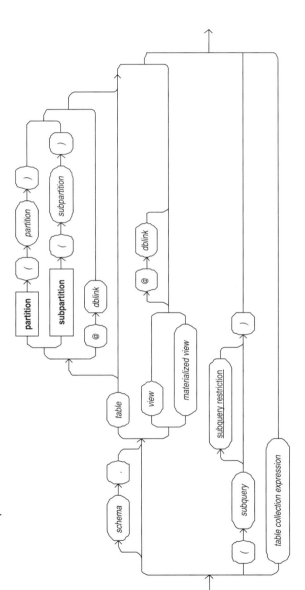

Subquery restriction

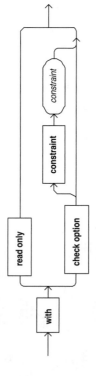

Table collection expression

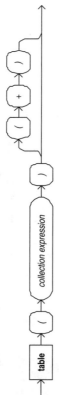

LOCK TABLE

Locks one or more tables, overriding automatic locking.

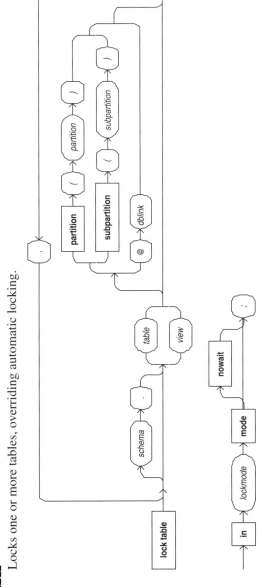

MERGE

Insert or update rows in one table based on a selection from another table.

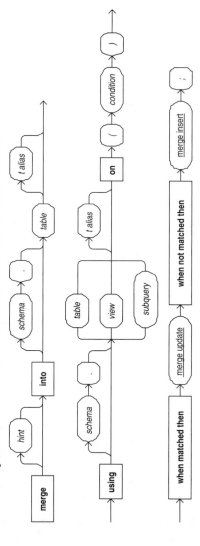

Merge update

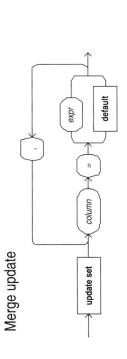

Merge insert

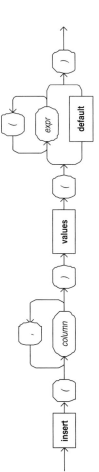

NOAUDIT

Stop auditing a particular audit statement.

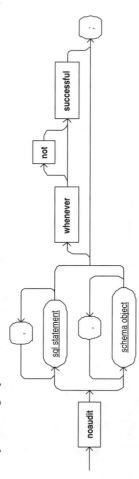

SQL statement

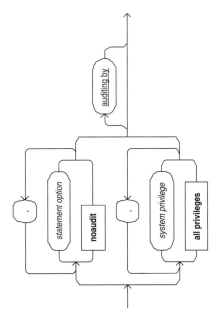

Auditing by

Auditing on

Schema object

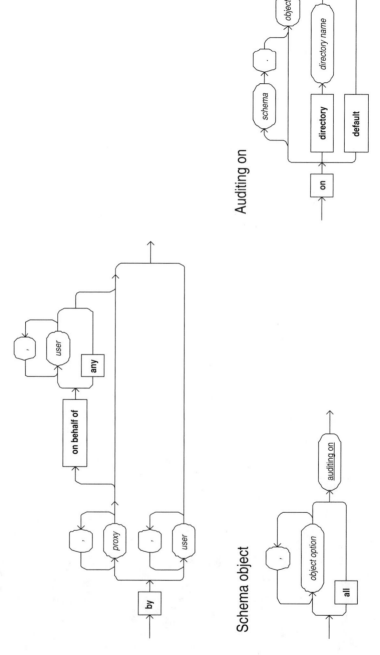

RENAME

Change the name of a table, view, sequence or private synonym.

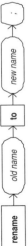

REVOKE

Remove a privilege, role or grant from a user or role.

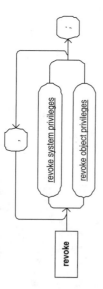

Revoke system privileges

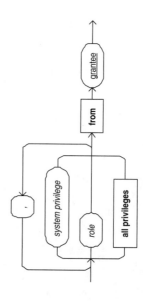

Revoke object privileges

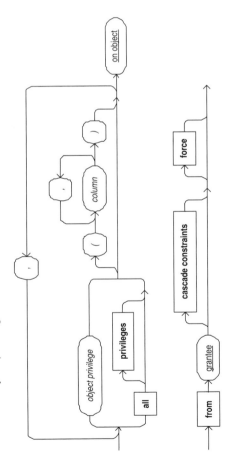

On object

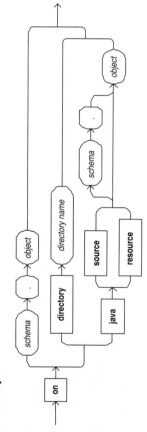

Grantee

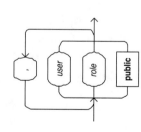

ROLLBACK

Undo the current transaction.

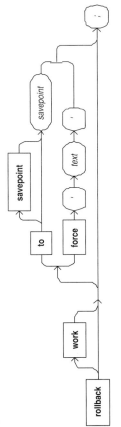

SAVEPOINT

Create a point in a transaction that can be rolled back to without rolling back the entire transaction.

SELECT

Retrieve data from the database.

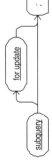

Subquery

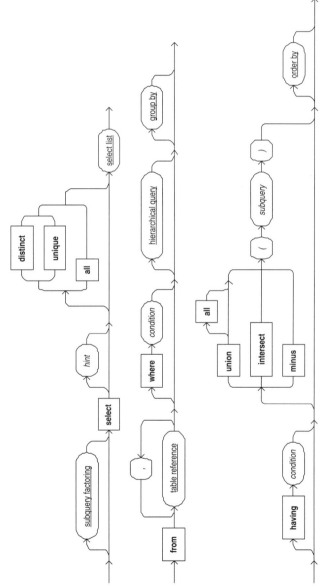

Subquery factoring

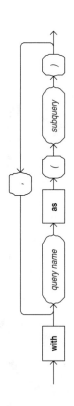

Select list

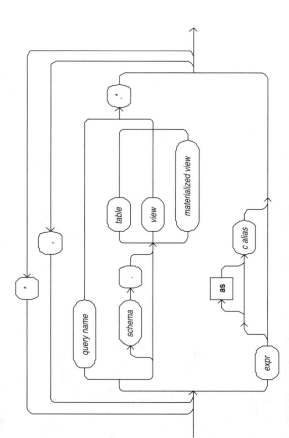

Table reference

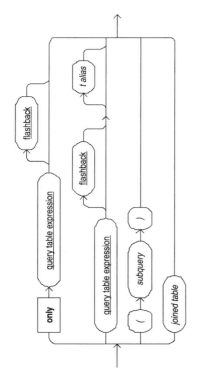

Flashback

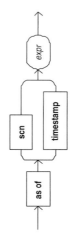

Query table expression

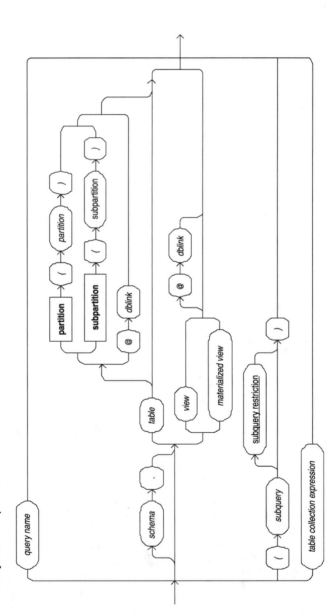

Sample

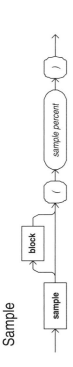

Subquery restriction

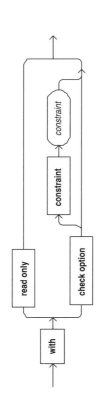

Table collection expression

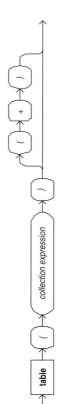

Joined table

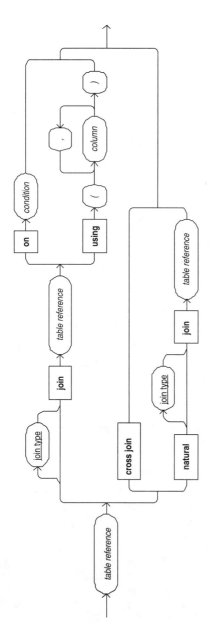

Join type

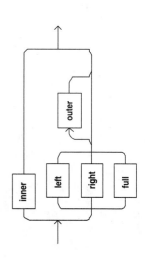

Hierarchical query

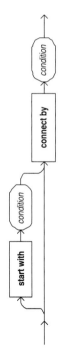

Group by

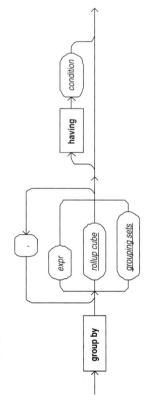

Rollup cube

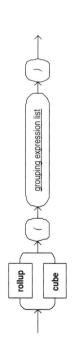

Grouping sets

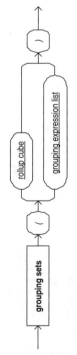

Grouping expression list

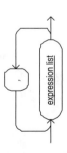

Expression list

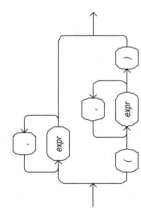

Order by

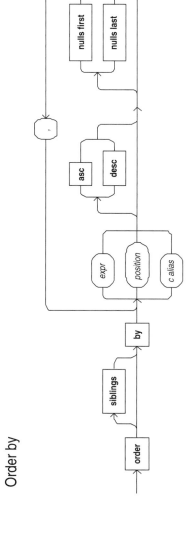

For update

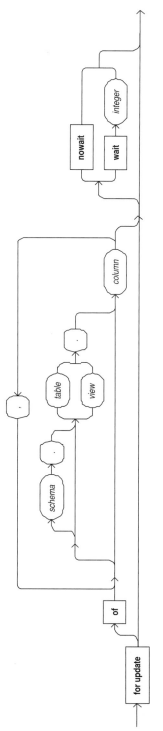

SET CONSTRAINT[S]

Specify for a specific transaction if deferrable constraints are checked. Can be in either form SET CONSTRAINT or SET CONSTRAINTS.

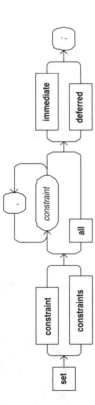

SET ROLE

Enable or disable roles for the current session.

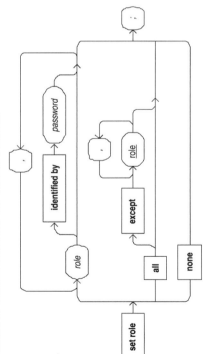

SET TRANSACTION

Change the parameters for the current transaction.

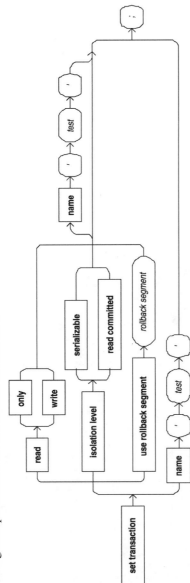

TRUNCATE

Remove all rows from a table or cluster. Can not be rolled back.

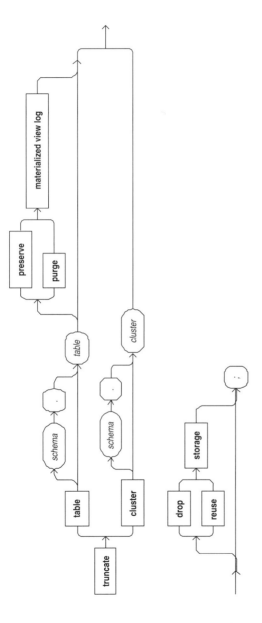

UPDATE

Change existing values in a table.

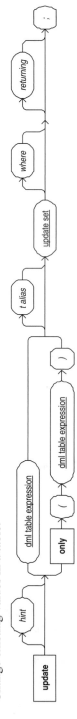

DML table expression

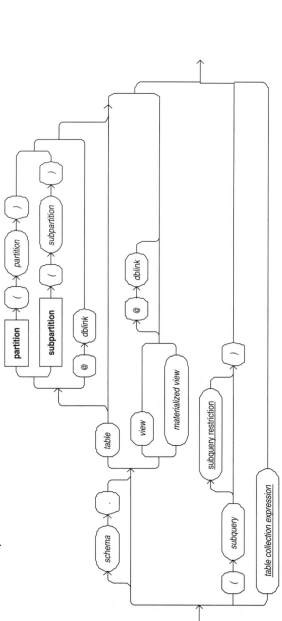

Subquery restriction

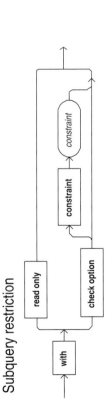

Table collection expression

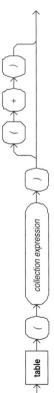

Update set

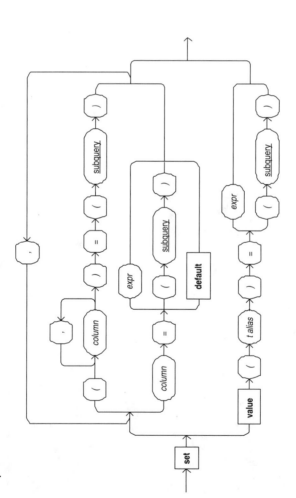

Where

Returning

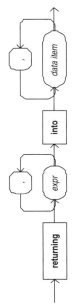

COMMON

Routines and syntax shared by multiple commands.

Allocate extent

Syntax of allocate extent statements.

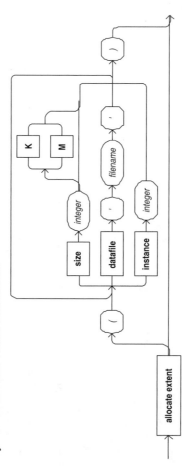

Constraints

Syntax for setting constraints on an object.

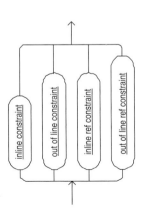

Inline constraint

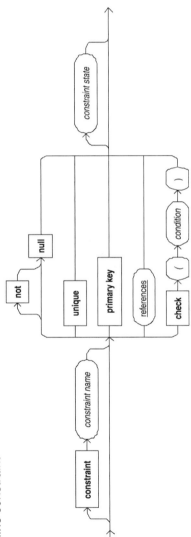

Out of line constraint

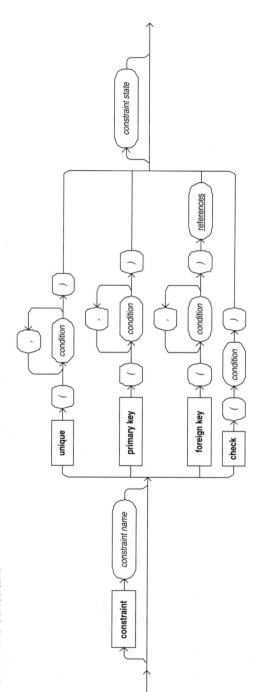

Inline ref constraint

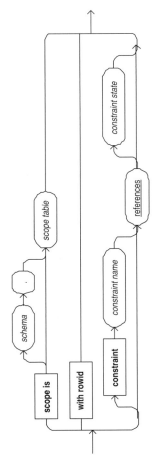

Out of line ref constraint

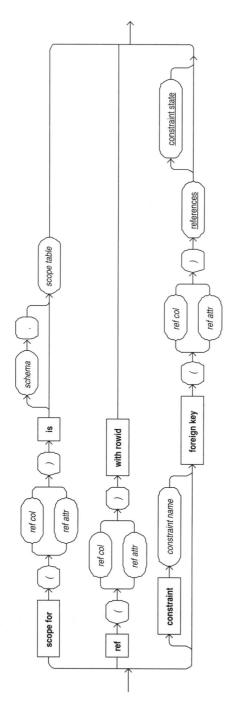

References

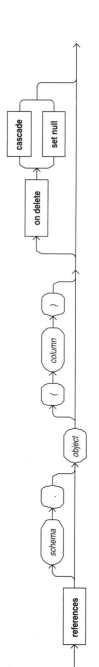

Constraint state

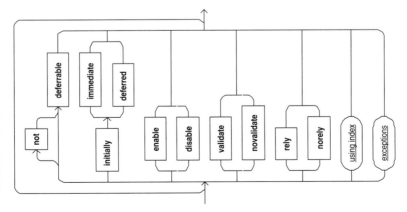

Using index

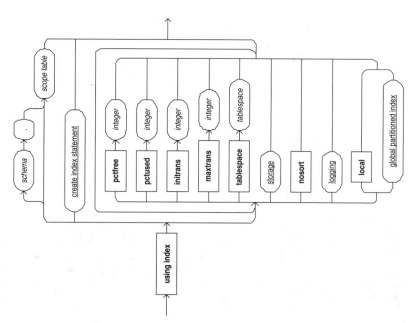

Global partitioned index

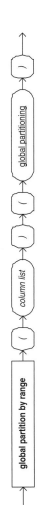

Index partitioning

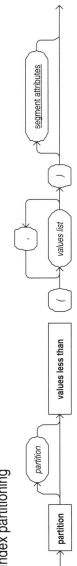

Segment attributes

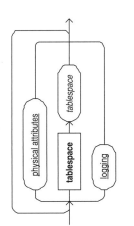

Physical attributes

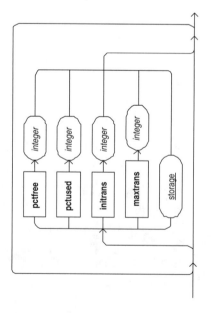

Exceptions

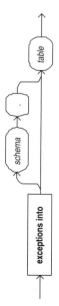

Deallocate Unused

Syntax for Deallocating Unused Space.

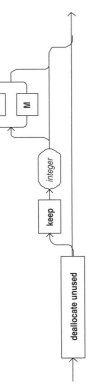

File Specification

Syntax for setting file specifications of database objects.

Datafile tempfile spec

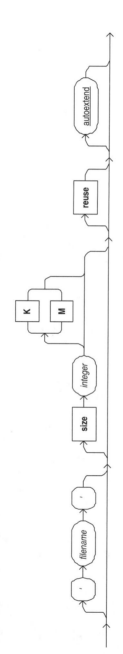

Redo log file spec

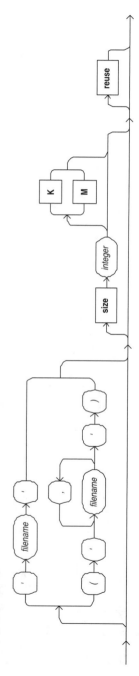

Autoextend

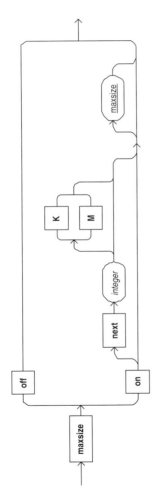

Maxsize

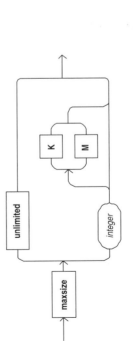

Logging

Syntax for common logging specifications.

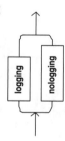

Parallel

Syntax for parallel options.

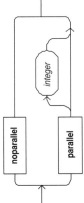

Physical Attributes

Syntax for common physical attributes of the database and its objects.

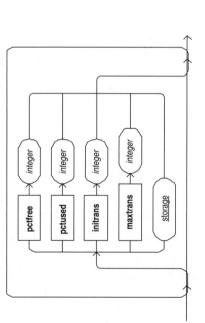

Storage

Syntax for setting storage parameters of the database.

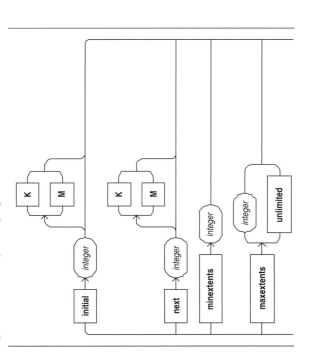

Storage (cont.)

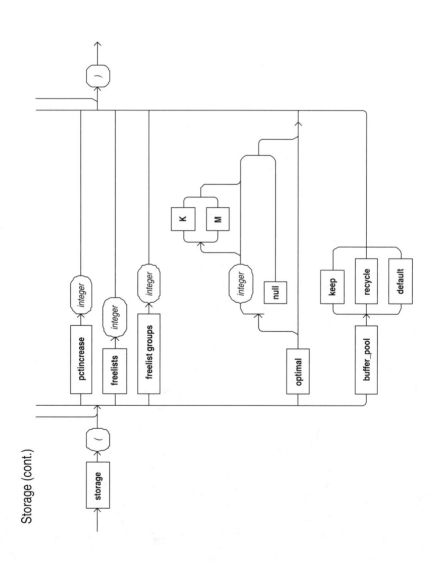

Chapter Three

Special Views and Tables

A listing of the special tables and views that are available to users and DBAs.

DATA DICTIONARY VIEWS

Oracle provides a rich set of data dictionary views. These views are owned by the user "SYS" and can be accessed by suitably privileged users. Views that begin with USER_ do not include an OWNER column, since they describe only the objects owned by the currently logged in user.

To get a list of these views, from the database, and the comments associated with them, log on to SQL*Plus as sysdba (internal) and then execute the following package to install it:

```
CREATE OR REPLACE PACKAGE describe
IS

    PROCEDURE describe_tables( tab_owner VARCHAR2, names_like VARCHAR2 ) ;
END describe;
/

CREATE OR REPLACE PACKAGE BODY describe
IS
```

```
PROCEDURE print_preamble
IS
BEGIN
    dbms_output.put_line( '<HTML>' );
    dbms_output.put_line( '<HEAD>' );
    dbms_output.put_line( '<TITLE>' );
    dbms_output.put_line( 'Table and Column Descriptions and Comments' );
    dbms_output.put_line( '</TITLE>' );
    dbms_output.put_line( '</HEAD>' );
    dbms_output.put_line( '<BODY>' );
    dbms_output.put_line( '<TABLE BORDER=1>' );
END;

PROCEDURE print_postamble
IS
BEGIN
    dbms_output.put_line( '</TABLE>' );
    dbms_output.put_line( '</BODY>' );
END;

PROCEDURE describe_tables( tab_owner VARCHAR2, names_like VARCHAR2 )
IS
    CURSOR tabs( tab_owner VARCHAR2, names_like VARCHAR2 )
    IS
        SELECT table_name,
               comments
          FROM dba_tab_comments
         WHERE owner = tab_owner
           AND table_name LIKE names_like
         ORDER BY table_name;
```

```
CURSOR cols( tab_owner VARCHAR2, tab_name VARCHAR2 )
IS
    SELECT a.column_name,
           a.comments,
           DECODE(b.data_type,
                  'BLOB', 'BLOB',
                  'CHAR', 'CHAR ('||b.data_length||')',
                  'CLOB', 'CLOB',
                  'DATE', 'DATE',
                  'FLOAT', 'FLOAT '||
                       DECODE( NVL( b.data_precision, 0 ), 0, NULL,
                           '('||b.data_precision||','||b.data_scale||')' ),
                  'LONG', 'LONG',
                  'LONG RAW', 'LONG RAW',
                  'MLSLABEL', 'MLSLABEL',
                  'NCHAR', 'NCHAR ('||b.data_length||')',
                  'NCLOB', 'NCLOB',
                  'NUMBER', 'NUMBER '||
                       DECODE( NVL( b.data_precision, 0 ), 0, NULL,
                           '('||b.data_precision||','||b.data_scale||')' ),
                  'NVARCHAR2', 'NVARCHAR2 ('||b.data_length||')',
                  'RAW', 'RAW ('||b.data_length||')',
                  'ROWID', 'ROWID',
                  'VARCHAR2', 'VARCHAR2 ('||b.data_length||')',
                  'UNKNOWN' ) col_type,
           decode( b.nullable, 'N', 'NOT NULL', NULL ) null_str,
           b.data_default
    FROM dba_col_comments a, dba_tab_columns b
    WHERE a.owner = tab_owner
```

```
        AND a.table_name = tab_name
        AND a.owner = b.owner
        AND a.table_name = b.table_name
        AND a.column_name = b.column_name
        ORDER by b.column_id;
BEGIN
    print_preamble;

    FOR tab_rec IN tabs( tab_owner, names_like )
    LOOP
        dbms_output.put_line( '<TR><TD>'||
                            tab_rec.table_name||
                            '</TD><TD>'||
                            tab_rec.comments||
                            '</TD></TR>'
                            );

        dbms_output.put_line( '<TR><TABLE>' );

        FOR col_rec IN cols( tab_owner, tab_rec.table_name )
        LOOP
            dbms_output.put_line( '<TR><TD>'||
                                col_rec.column_name||
                                '</TD><TD>'||
                                col_rec.col_type||
                                '</TD><TD>'||
                                col_rec.null_str||
                                '</TD><TD>'||
                                col_rec.data_default||
                                '</TD><TD>'||
```

```
                  col_rec.comments||
                  '</TD></TR>'
          );

   END LOOP;

   dbms_output.put_line( '</TR></TABLE>' );
   END LOOP;

   print_postamble;
   END;
END describe;
/
```

Then to run the package, from the SQL> prompt:

```
set serveroutput on 1000000
exec describe.describe_tables('SYS','DBA_%')
```

the output will scroll to the screen unless you set a spool.

Table 3-1   Data Dictionary Views

_ALL_INSTANTIATION_DDL	_ALL_REPCOLUMN	_ALL_REPCOLUMN_GROUP
_ALL_REPCONFLICT	_ALL_REPEXTENSIONS	_ALL_REPFLAVOR_OBJECTS
_ALL_REPGROUPED_COLUMN	_ALL_REPPARAMETER_COLUMN	_ALL_REPRESOLUTION
_ALL_REPSITES_NEW	ALL_ALL_TABLES	ALL_APPLY
ALL_APPLY_CONFLICT_COLUMNS	ALL_APPLY_DML_HANDLERS	ALL_APPLY_ERROR
ALL_APPLY_KEY_COLUMNS	ALL_APPLY_PARAMETERS	ALL_APPLY_PROGRESS
ALL_ARGUMENTS	ALL_ASSOCIATIONS	ALL_AUDIT_POLICIES

Table 3-1 Data Dictionary Views (continued)

ALL_INSTANTIATION_DDL	ALL_REPCOLUMN	ALL_REPCOLUMN_GROUP
ALL_BASE_TABLE_MVIEWS	ALL_CAPTURE	ALL_CAPTURE_PARAMETERS
ALL_CAPTURE_PREPARED_DATABASE	ALL_CAPTURE_PREPARED_SCHEMAS	ALL_CAPTURE_PREPARED_TABLES
ALL_CATALOG	ALL_CLUSTER_HASH_EXPRESSIONS	ALL_CLUSTERS
ALL_COL_COMMENTS	ALL_COL_PRIVS	ALL_COL_PRIVS_MADE
ALL_COL_PRIVS_RECD	ALL_COLL_TYPES	ALL_CONS_COLUMNS
ALL_CONS_OBJ_COLUMNS	ALL_CONSTRAINTS	ALL_CONTEXT
ALL_DB_LINKS	ALL_DEF_AUDIT_OPTS	ALL_DEPENDENCIES
ALL_DIM_ATTRIBUTES	ALL_DIM_CHILD_OF	ALL_DIM_HIERARCHIES
ALL_DIM_JOIN_KEY	ALL_DIM_LEVEL_KEY	ALL_DIM_LEVELS
ALL_DIMENSIONS	ALL_DIRECTORIES	ALL_ERRORS
ALL_EVALUATION_CONTEXT_TABLES	ALL_EVALUATION_CONTEXT_VARS	ALL_EVALUATION_CONTEXTS
ALL_EXTERNAL_LOCATIONS	ALL_EXTERNAL_TABLES	ALL_IND_COLUMNS
ALL_IND_EXPRESSIONS	ALL_INDEXES	ALL_INDEXTYPE_COMMENTS
ALL_INDEXTYPE_OPERATORS	ALL_INDEXTYPES	ALL_INTERNAL_TRIGGERS
ALL_JAVA_ARGUMENTS	ALL_JAVA_CLASSES	ALL_JAVA_DERIVATIONS
ALL_JAVA_FIELDS	ALL_JAVA_IMPLEMENTS	ALL_JAVA_INNERS
ALL_JAVA_LAYOUTS	ALL_JAVA_METHODS	ALL_JAVA_NCOMPS
ALL_JAVA_RESOLVERS	ALL_JAVA_THROWS	ALL_JOIN_IND_COLUMNS
ALL_LIBRARIES	ALL_LOBS	ALL_LOG_GROUP_COLUMNS
ALL_LOG_GROUPS	ALL_METHOD_PARAMS	ALL_METHOD_RESULTS

Table 3-1 Data Dictionary Views (continued)

ALL_INSTANTIATION_DDL	ALL_REPCOLUMN	ALL_REPCOLUMN_GROUP
ALL_MVIEW_AGGREGATES	ALL_MVIEW_ANALYSIS	ALL_MVIEW_DETAIL_RELATIONS
ALL_MVIEW_JOINS	ALL_MVIEW_KEYS	ALL_MVIEW_LOGS
ALL_MVIEW_REFRESH_TIMES	ALL_MVIEWS	ALL_NESTED_TABLES
ALL_OBJ_COLATTRS	ALL_OBJECT_TABLES	ALL_OBJECTS
ALL_OPANCILLARY	ALL_OPARGUMENTS	ALL_OPBINDINGS
ALL_OPERATOR_COMMENTS	ALL_OPERATORS	ALL_PARTIAL_DROP_TABS
ALL_PENDING_CONV_TABLES	ALL_POLICIES	ALL_POLICY_CONTEXTS
ALL_POLICY_GROUPS	ALL_PROCEDURES	ALL_PROPAGATION
ALL_QUEUE_TABLES	ALL_QUEUES	ALL_REFRESH
ALL_REFRESH_CHILDREN	ALL_REFRESH_DEPENDENCIES	ALL_REFS
ALL_REGISTERED_MVIEWS	ALL_REGISTERED_SNAPSHOTS	ALL_REPAUDIT_ATTRIBUTE
ALL_REPAUDIT_COLUMN	ALL_REPCATLOG	ALL_REPCOLUMN
ALL_REPCOLUMN_GROUP	ALL_REPCONFLICT	ALL_REPDDL
ALL_REPFLAVOR_COLUMNS	ALL_REPFLAVOR_OBJECTS	ALL_REPFLAVORS
ALL_REPGENERATED	ALL_REPGENOBJECTS	ALL_REPGROUP
ALL_REPGROUP_PRIVILEGES	ALL_REPGROUPED_COLUMN	ALL_REPKEY_COLUMNS
ALL_REPOBJECT	ALL_REPPARAMETER_COLUMN	ALL_REPPRIORITY
ALL_REPPRIORITY_GROUP	ALL_REPPROP	ALL_REPRESOL_STATS_CONTROL
ALL_REPRESOLUTION	ALL_REPRESOLUTION_METHOD	ALL_REPRESOLUTION_STATISTICS
ALL_REPSCHEMA	ALL_REPSITES	ALL_RULE_SET_RULES

Table 3-1 Data Dictionary Views (continued)

ALL_INSTANTIATION_DDL	ALL_REPCOLUMN	ALL_REPCOLUMN_GROUP
ALL_RULE_SETS	ALL_RULES	ALL_RULESETS
ALL_SECONDARY_OBJECTS	ALL_SEQUENCES	ALL_SNAPSHOT_LOGS
ALL_SNAPSHOTS	ALL_SOURCE	ALL_SQLJ_TYPE_ATTRS
ALL_SQLJ_TYPE_METHODS	ALL_SQLJ_TYPES	ALL_STORED_SETTINGS
ALL_STREAMS_GLOBAL_RULES	ALL_STREAMS_SCHEMA_RULES	ALL_STREAMS_TABLE_RULES
ALL_SUMDELTA	ALL_SUMMARIES	ALL_SYNONYMS
ALL_TAB_COL_STATISTICS	ALL_TAB_COLS	ALL_TAB_COLUMNS
ALL_TAB_COMMENTS	ALL_TAB_HISTOGRAMS	ALL_TAB_MODIFICATIONS
ALL_TAB_PRIVS	ALL_TAB_PRIVS_MADE	ALL_TAB_PRIVS_RECD
ALL_TABLES	ALL_TRIGGER_COLS	ALL_TRIGGERS
ALL_TYPE_ATTRS	ALL_TYPE_METHODS	ALL_TYPE_VERSIONS
ALL_TYPES	ALL_UNUSED_COL_TABS	ALL_UPDATABLE_COLUMNS
ALL_USERS	ALL_USTATS	ALL_VARRAYS
ALL_VIEWS	ALL_XML_SCHEMAS	ALL_XML_TAB_COLS
ALL_XML_TABLES	ALL_XML_VIEW_COLS	ALL_XML_VIEWS
ATEMPTAB$	AUDIT_ACTIONS	COLUMN_PRIVILEGES
DATABASE_COMPATIBLE_LEVEL	DATABASE_PROPERTIES	DBA_2PC_NEIGHBORS
DBA_2PC_PENDING	DBA_ALL_TABLES	DBA_APPLY
DBA_APPLY_CONFLICT_COLUMNS	DBA_APPLY_DML_HANDLERS	DBA_APPLY_ERROR
DBA_APPLY_INSTANTIATED_OBJECTS	DBA_APPLY_KEY_COLUMNS	DBA_APPLY_PARAMETERS

Table 3-1 Data Dictionary Views (continued)

_ALL_INSTANTIATION_DDL	_ALL_REPCOLUMN	_ALL_REPCOLUMN_GROUP
DBA_APPLY_PROGRESS	DBA_ASSOCIATIONS	DBA_AUDIT_EXISTS
DBA_AUDIT_OBJECT	DBA_AUDIT_POLICIES	DBA_AUDIT_SESSION
DBA_AUDIT_STATEMENT	DBA_AUDIT_TRAIL	DBA_AW_PS
DBA_AWS	DBA_BASE_TABLE_MVIEWS	DBA_CAPTURE
DBA_CAPTURE_PARAMETERS	DBA_CAPTURE_PREPARED_DATABASE	DBA_CAPTURE_PREPARED_SCHEMAS
DBA_CAPTURE_PREPARED_TABLES	DBA_CATALOG	DBA_CLU_COLUMNS
DBA_CLUSTER_HASH_EXPRESSIONS	DBA_CLUSTERS	DBA_COL_COMMENTS
DBA_COL_PRIVS	DBA_COLL_TYPES	DBA_CONS_COLUMNS
DBA_CONS_OBJ_COLUMNS	DBA_CONSTRAINTS	DBA_CONTEXT
DBA_DATA_FILES	DBA_DB_LINKS	DBA_DEPENDENCIES
DBA_DIM_ATTRIBUTES	DBA_DIM_CHILD_OF	DBA_DIM_HIERARCHIES
DBA_DIM_JOIN_KEY	DBA_DIM_LEVEL_KEY	DBA_DIM_LEVELS
DBA_DIMENSIONS	DBA_DIRECTORIES	DBA_DMT_FREE_SPACE
DBA_DMT_USED_EXTENTS	DBA_ERRORS	DBA_EVALUATION_CONTEXT_TABLES
DBA_EVALUATION_CONTEXT_VARS	DBA_EVALUATION_CONTEXTS	DBA_EXP_FILES
DBA_EXP_OBJECTS	DBA_EXP_VERSION	DBA_EXTENTS
DBA_EXTERNAL_LOCATIONS	DBA_EXTERNAL_TABLES	DBA_FGA_AUDIT_TRAIL
DBA_FREE_SPACE	DBA_FREE_SPACE_COALESCED	DBA_GLOBAL_CONTEXT
DBA_IND_COLUMNS	DBA_IND_EXPRESSIONS	DBA_INDEXES
DBA_INDEXTYPE_COMMENTS	DBA_INDEXTYPE_OPERATORS	DBA_INDEXTYPES

Table 3-1   Data Dictionary Views (continued)

ALL_INSTANTIATION_DDL	ALL_REPCOLUMN	ALL_REPCOLUMN_GROUP
DBA_INTERNAL_TRIGGERS	DBA_JAVA_ARGUMENTS	DBA_JAVA_CLASSES
DBA_JAVA_DERIVATIONS	DBA_JAVA_FIELDS	DBA_JAVA_IMPLEMENTS
DBA_JAVA_INNERS	DBA_JAVA_LAYOUTS	DBA_JAVA_METHODS
DBA_JAVA_POLICY	DBA_JAVA_RESOLVERS	DBA_JAVA_THROWS
DBA_JOBS	DBA_JOBS_RUNNING	DBA_JOIN_IND_COLUMNS
DBA_LIBRARIES	DBA_LMT_FREE_SPACE	DBA_LMT_USED_EXTENTS
DBA_LOBS	DBA_LOG_GROUP_COLUMNS	DBA_LOG_GROUPS
DBA_LOGSTDBY_EVENTS	DBA_LOGSTDBY_NOT_UNIQUE	DBA_LOGSTDBY_PARAMETERS
DBA_LOGSTDBY_PROGRESS	DBA_LOGSTDBY_SKIP	DBA_LOGSTDBY_SKIP_TRANSACTION
DBA_LOGSTDBY_UNSUPPORTED	DBA_METHOD_PARAMS	DBA_METHOD_RESULTS
DBA_MVIEW_AGGREGATES	DBA_MVIEW_ANALYSIS	DBA_MVIEW_DETAIL_RELATIONS
DBA_MVIEW_JOINS	DBA_MVIEW_KEYS	DBA_MVIEW_LOG_FILTER_COLS
DBA_MVIEW_LOGS	DBA_MVIEW_REFRESH_TIMES	DBA_MVIEWS
DBA_NESTED_TABLES	DBA_OBJ_AUDIT_OPTS	DBA_OBJ_COLATTRS
DBA_OBJECT_SIZE	DBA_OBJECT_TABLES	DBA_OBJECTS
DBA_OPANCILLARY	DBA_OPARGUMENTS	DBA_OPBINDINGS
DBA_OPERATOR_COMMENTS	DBA_OPERATORS	DBA_OUTLINE_HINTS
DBA_OUTLINES	DBA_PARTIAL_DROP_TABS	DBA_PENDING_CONV_TABLES
DBA_PENDING_TRANSACTIONS	DBA_POLICIES	DBA_POLICY_CONTEXTS
DBA_POLICY_GROUPS	DBA_PRIV_AUDIT_OPTS	DBA_PROCEDURES

Table 3-1   Data Dictionary Views (continued)

ALL_INSTANTIATION_DDL	ALL_REPCOLUMN	ALL_REPCOLUMN_GROUP
DBA_PROFILES	DBA_PROPAGATION	DBA_PROXIES
DBA_QUEUE_TABLES	DBA_QUEUES	DBA_RCHILD
DBA_REFRESH	DBA_REFRESH_CHILDREN	DBA_REFS
DBA_REGISTERED_MVIEW_GROUPS	DBA_REGISTERED_MVIEWS	DBA_REGISTERED_SNAPSHOT_GROUPS
DBA_REGISTERED_SNAPSHOTS	DBA_REPAUDIT_ATTRIBUTE	DBA_REPAUDIT_COLUMN
DBA_REPCAT_EXCEPTIONS	DBA_REPCATLOG	DBA_REPCOLUMN
DBA_REPCOLUMN_GROUP	DBA_REPCONFLICT	DBA_REPDDL
DBA_REPEXTENSIONS	DBA_REPFLAVOR_COLUMNS	DBA_REPFLAVOR_OBJECTS
DBA_REPFLAVORS	DBA_REPGENERATED	DBA_REPGENOBJECTS
DBA_REPGROUP	DBA_REPGROUP_PRIVILEGES	DBA_REPGROUPED_COLUMN
DBA_REPKEY_COLUMNS	DBA_REPOBJECT	DBA_REPPARAMETER_COLUMN
DBA_REPPRIORITY	DBA_REPPRIORITY_GROUP	DBA_REPPROP
DBA_REPRESOL_STATS_CONTROL	DBA_REPRESOLUTION	DBA_REPRESOLUTION_METHOD
DBA_REPRESOLUTION_STATISTICS	DBA_REPSCHEMA	DBA_REPSITES
DBA_REPSITES_NEW	DBA_RESUMABLE	DBA_RGROUP
DBA_ROLE_PRIVS	DBA_ROLES	DBA_ROLLBACK_SEGS
DBA_RSRC_CONSUMER_GROUP_PRIVS	DBA_RSRC_CONSUMER_GROUPS	DBA_RSRC_MANAGER_SYSTEM_PRIVS
DBA_RSRC_PLAN_DIRECTIVES	DBA_RSRC_PLANS	DBA_RULE_SET_RULES
DBA_RULE_SETS	DBA_RULES	DBA_RULESETS
DBA_SECONDARY_OBJECTS	DBA_SEGMENTS	DBA_SEQUENCES

Table 3-1 Data Dictionary Views (continued)

_ALL_INSTANTIATION_DDL	_ALL_REPCOLUMN	_ALL_REPCOLUMN_GROUP
DBA_SNAPSHOT_LOGS	DBA_SNAPSHOTS	DBA_SOURCE
DBA_SQLJ_TYPE_ATTRS	DBA_SQLJ_TYPE_METHODS	DBA_SQLJ_TYPES
DBA_STMT_AUDIT_OPTS	DBA_STORED_SETTINGS	DBA_STREAMS_GLOBAL_RULES
DBA_STREAMS_SCHEMA_RULES	DBA_STREAMS_TABLE_RULES	DBA_SUMMARIES
DBA_SYNONYMS	DBA_SYS_PRIVS	DBA_TAB_COL_STATISTICS
DBA_TAB_COLS	DBA_TAB_COLUMNS	DBA_TAB_COMMENTS
DBA_TAB_HISTOGRAMS	DBA_TAB_MODIFICATIONS	DBA_TAB_PRIVS
DBA_TABLES	DBA_TABLESPACES	DBA_TEMP_FILES
DBA_TEMPLATE_REFGROUPS	DBA_TEMPLATE_TARGETS	DBA_TRIGGER_COLS
DBA_TRIGGERS	DBA_TS_QUOTAS	DBA_TYPE_ATTRS
DBA_TYPE_METHODS	DBA_TYPE_VERSIONS	DBA_TYPES
DBA_UNDO_EXTENTS	DBA_UNUSED_COL_TABS	DBA_UPDATABLE_COLUMNS
DBA_USERS	DBA_USTATS	DBA_VARRAYS
DBA_VIEWS	DBA_XML_SCHEMAS	DBA_XML_TAB_COLS
DBA_XML_TABLES	DBA_XML_VIEW_COLS	DBA_XML_VIEWS
DEFCALL	DEFCALLDEST	DEFDEFAULTDEST
DEFERRCOUNT	DEFERROR	DEFLOB
DEFPROPAGATOR	DEFSCHEDULE	DEFTRAN
DICT_COLUMNS	DICTIONARY	FILEXT$
GLOBAL_CONTEXT	GLOBAL_NAME	INDEX_HISTOGRAM

Table 3-1 Data Dictionary Views (continued)

ALL_INSTANTIATION_DDL	ALL_REPCOLUMN	ALL_REPCOLUMN_GROUP
INDEX_STATS	NLS_DATABASE_PARAMETERS	NLS_INSTANCE_PARAMETERS
NLS_SESSION_PARAMETERS	PRODUCT_COMPONENT_VERSION	PROXY_ROLES
PROXY_USERS	PROXY_USERS_AND_ROLES	PUBLIC_DEPENDENCY
QUEUE_PRIVILEGES	REPCAT_GENERATED	REPCAT_REPCAT
REPCAT_REPCATLOG	REPCAT_REPCOLUMN_BASE	REPCAT_REPFLAVOR_COLUMNS
REPCAT_REPOBJECT	REPCAT_REPOBJECT_BASE	REPCAT_REPPROP
REPCAT_REPSCHEMA	RESOURCE_COST	RESOURCE_MAP
ROLE_ROLE_PRIVS	ROLE_SYS_PRIVS	ROLE_TAB_PRIVS
SESSION_CONTEXT	SESSION_PRIVS	SESSION_ROLES
STMT_AUDIT_OPTION_MAP	SYSTEM_PRIVILEGE_MAP	TABLE_PRIVILEGE_MAP
TABLE_PRIVILEGES	TRUSTED_SERVERS	USER_ALL_TABLES
USER_ARGUMENTS	USER_ASSOCIATIONS	USER_AUDIT_OBJECT
USER_AUDIT_POLICIES	USER_AUDIT_SESSION	USER_AUDIT_STATEMENT
USER_AUDIT_TRAIL	USER_AW_PS	USER_AWS
USER_BASE_TABLE_MVIEWS	USER_CATALOG	USER_CLU_COLUMNS
USER_CLUSTER_HASH_EXPRESSIONS	USER_CLUSTERS	USER_COL_COMMENTS
USER_COL_PRIVS	USER_COL_PRIVS_MADE	USER_COL_PRIVS_RECD
USER_COLL_TYPES	USER_CONS_COLUMNS	USER_CONS_OBJ_COLUMNS
USER_CONSTRAINTS	USER_DB_LINKS	USER_DEPENDENCIES
USER_DIM_ATTRIBUTES	USER_DIM_CHILD_OF	USER_DIM_HIERARCHIES

Table 3-1   Data Dictionary Views (continued)

ALL_INSTANTIATION_DDL	ALL_REPCOLUMN	ALL_REPCOLUMN_GROUP
USER_DIM_JOIN_KEY	USER_DIM_LEVEL_KEY	USER_DIM_LEVELS
USER_DIMENSIONS	USER_ERRORS	USER_EVALUATION_CONTEXT_TABLES
USER_EVALUATION_CONTEXT_VARS	USER_EVALUATION_CONTEXTS	USER_EXTENTS
USER_EXTERNAL_LOCATIONS	USER_EXTERNAL_TABLES	USER_FREE_SPACE
USER_IND_COLUMNS	USER_IND_EXPRESSIONS	USER_INDEXES
USER_INDEXTYPE_COMMENTS	USER_INDEXTYPE_OPERATORS	USER_INDEXTYPES
USER_INTERNAL_TRIGGERS	USER_JAVA_ARGUMENTS	USER_JAVA_CLASSES
USER_JAVA_DERIVATIONS	USER_JAVA_FIELDS	USER_JAVA_IMPLEMENTS
USER_JAVA_INNERS	USER_JAVA_LAYOUTS	USER_JAVA_METHODS
USER_JAVA_NCOMPS	USER_JAVA_POLICY	USER_JAVA_RESOLVERS
USER_JAVA_THROWS	USER_JOBS	USER_JOIN_IND_COLUMNS
USER_LIBRARIES	USER_LOBS	USER_LOG_GROUP_COLUMNS
USER_LOG_GROUPS	USER_METHOD_PARAMS	USER_METHOD_RESULTS
USER_MVIEW_AGGREGATES	USER_MVIEW_ANALYSIS	USER_MVIEW_DETAIL_RELATIONS
USER_MVIEW_JOINS	USER_MVIEW_KEYS	USER_MVIEW_LOGS
USER_MVIEW_REFRESH_TIMES	USER_MVIEWS	USER_NESTED_TABLES
USER_OBJ_AUDIT_OPTS	USER_OBJ_COLATTRS	USER_OBJECT_SIZE
USER_OBJECT_TABLES	USER_OBJECTS	USER_OPANCILLARY
USER_OPARGUMENTS	USER_OPBINDINGS	USER_OPERATOR_COMMENTS
USER_OPERATORS	USER_OUTLINE_HINTS	USER_OUTLINES

Table 3-1 Data Dictionary Views (continued)

ALL_INSTANTIATION_DDL	ALL_REPCOLUMN	ALL_REPCOLUMN_GROUP
USER_PARTIAL_DROP_TABS	USER_PASSWORD_LIMITS	USER_PENDING_CONV_TABLES
USER_POLICIES	USER_POLICY_CONTEXTS	USER_POLICY_GROUPS
USER_PROCEDURES	USER_PROXIES	USER_QUEUE_TABLES
USER_QUEUES	USER_REFRESH	USER_REFRESH_CHILDREN
USER_REFS	USER_REGISTERED_MVIEWS	USER_REGISTERED_SNAPSHOTS
USER_REPAUDIT_ATTRIBUTE	USER_REPAUDIT_COLUMN	USER_REPCATLOG
USER_REPCOLUMN	USER_REPCOLUMN_GROUP	USER_REPDDL
USER_REPFLAVOR_COLUMNS	USER_REPFLAVOR_OBJECTS	USER_REPFLAVORS
USER_REPGENERATED	USER_REPGENOBJECTS	USER_REPGROUP
USER_REPGROUP_PRIVILEGES	USER_REPGROUPED_COLUMN	USER_REPKEY_COLUMNS
USER_REPOBJECT	USER_REPPARAMETER_COLUMN	USER_REPPRIORITY
USER_REPPRIORITY_GROUP	USER_REPPROP	USER_REPRESOL_STATS_CONTROL
USER_REPRESOLUTION	USER_REPRESOLUTION_METHOD	USER_REPRESOLUTION_STATISTICS
USER_REPSCHEMA	USER_REPSITES	USER_RESOURCE_LIMITS
USER_RESUMABLE	USER_ROLE_PRIVS	USER_RSRC_CONSUMER_GROUP_PRIVS
USER_RSRC_MANAGER_SYSTEM_PRIVS	USER_RULE_SET_RULES	USER_RULE_SETS
USER_RULES	USER_RULESETS	USER_SECONDARY_OBJECTS
USER_SEGMENTS	USER_SEQUENCES	USER_SNAPSHOT_LOGS
USER_SOURCE	USER_SOURCE	USER_SQLJ_TYPE_ATTRS
USER_SQLJ_TYPE_METHODS	USER_SQLJ_TYPES	USER_STORED_SETTINGS

Table 3-1 Data Dictionary Views (continued)

_ALL_INSTANTIATION_DDL	_ALL_REPCOLUMN	_ALL_REPCOLUMN_GROUP
USER_SUMMARIES	USER_SYNONYMS	USER_SYS_PRIVS
USER_TAB_COL_STATISTICS	USER_TAB_COLS	USER_TAB_COLUMNS
USER_TAB_COMMENTS	USER_TAB_HISTOGRAMS	USER_TAB_MODIFICATIONS
USER_TAB_PRIVS	USER_TAB_PRIVS_MADE	USER_TAB_PRIVS_RECD
USER_TABLES	USER_TABLESPACES	USER_TRIGGER_COLS
USER_TRIGGERS	USER_TS_QUOTAS	USER_TYPE_ATTRS
USER_TYPE_METHODS	USER_TYPE_VERSIONS	USER_TYPES
USER_UNUSED_COL_TABS	USER_UPDATABLE_COLUMNS	USER_USERS
USER_USTATS	USER_VARRAYS	USER_VIEWS
USER_XML_SCHEMAS	USER_XML_TAB_COLS	USER_XML_TABLES
USER_XML_VIEW_COLS	USER_XML_VIEWS	

DYNAMIC TABLES

Oracle provides dynamically populated performance tables, owned by SYS, that permit the DBA to view current information about a wide variety of conditions in the database. These tables are generally accessed via their public synonyms. In all cases except V$OBJECT_USAGE, where the two names are identical, the table name is the same as the synonym name, except for the insertion of an underscore character before the dollar sign. An example would be the public synonym of V$SQLXS for the table SYS.V_$SQLXS. Table 3-2 is a complete list of these synonyms, and Table 3-3 expands that list to show the columns in each of the underlying Views.

Table 3-2 Complete List of "V$" Synonyms

V$_LOCK	V$ACCESS
V$ACTIVE_INSTANCES	V$ACTIVE_SESS_POOL_MTH
V$AQ	V$AQ1
V$ARCHIVE	V$ARCHIVED_LOG
V$ARCHIVE_DEST	V$ARCHIVE_DEST_STATUS
V$ARCHIVE_GAP	V$ARCHIVE_PROCESSES
V$AW_CALC	V$AW_OLAP
V$AW_SESSION_INFO	V$BACKUP
V$BACKUP_ASYNC_IO	V$BACKUP_CORRUPTION
V$BACKUP_DATAFILE	V$BACKUP_DEVICE
V$BACKUP_PIECE	V$BACKUP_REDOLOG
V$BACKUP_SET	V$BACKUP_SPFILE
V$BACKUP_SYNC_IO	V$BGPROCESS
V$BH	V$BSP

Table 3-2 Complete List of "V$" Synonyms (continued)

V$BUFFER_POOL	V$BUFFER_POOL_STATISTICS
V$CIRCUIT	V$CLASS_CACHE_TRANSFER
V$CLASS_PING	V$COMPATIBILITY
V$COMPATSEG	V$CONTEXT
V$CONTROLFILE	V$CONTROLFILE_RECORD_SECTION
V$COPY_CORRUPTION	V$CR_BLOCK_SERVER
V$DATABASE	V$DATABASE_BLOCK_CORRUPTION
V$DATABASE_INCARNATION	V$DATAFILE
V$DATAFILE_COPY	V$DATAFILE_HEADER
V$DATAGUARD_STATUS	V$DBFILE
V$DBLINK	V$DB_CACHE_ADVICE
V$DB_OBJECT_CACHE	V$DB_PIPES
V$DELETED_OBJECT	V$DISPATCHER
V$DISPATCHER_RATE	V$DLM_ALL_LOCKS
V$DLM_CONVERT_LOCAL	V$DLM_CONVERT_REMOTE
V$DLM_LATCH	V$DLM_LOCKS
V$DLM_MISC	V$DLM_RESS
V$DLM_TRAFFIC_CONTROLLER	V$ENABLEDPRIVS
V$ENQUEUE_LOCK	V$ENQUEUE_STAT
V$EVENT_NAME	V$EXECUTION
V$FAST_START_SERVERS	V$FAST_START_TRANSACTIONS

Table 3-2   Complete List of "V$" Synonyms (continued)

V$FILESTAT	V$FILESTATXS
V$FILE_CACHE_TRANSFER	V$FILE_PING
V$FIXED_TABLE	V$FIXED_VIEW_DEFINITION
V$GCSHVMASTER_INFO	V$GCSPFMASTER_INFO
V$GC_ELEMENT	V$GC_ELEMENTS_WITH_COLLISIONS
V$GES_BLOCKING_ENQUEUE	V$GES_ENQUEUE
V$GLOBALCONTEXT	V$GLOBAL_BLOCKED_LOCKS
V$GLOBAL_TRANSACTION	V$HS_AGENT
V$HS_PARAMETER	V$HS_SESSION
V$HVMASTER_INFO	V$INDEXED_FIXED_COLUMN
V$INSTANCE	V$INSTANCE_RECOVERY
V$LATCH	V$LATCHHOLDER
V$LATCHNAME	V$LATCH_CHILDREN
V$LATCH_MISSES	V$LATCH_PARENT
V$LIBRARYCACHE	V$LIBRARY_CACHE_MEMORY
V$LICENSE	V$LOADISTAT
V$LOADPSTAT	V$LOCK
V$LOCKED_OBJECT	V$LOCKS_WITH_COLLISIONS
V$LOCK_ACTIVITY	V$LOCK_ELEMENT
V$LOG	V$LOGFILE
V$LOGHIST	V$LOGMNR_CALLBACK

Table 3-2   Complete List of "V$" Synonyms (continued)

V$LOGMNR_CONTENTS	V$LOGMNR_DICTIONARY
V$LOGMNR_LOGFILE	V$LOGMNR_LOGS
V$LOGMNR_PARAMETERS	V$LOGMNR_PROCESS
V$LOGMNR_REGION	V$LOGMNR_SESSION
V$LOGMNR_STATS	V$LOGMNR_TRANSACTION
V$LOGSTDBY	V$LOGSTDBY_STATS
V$LOG_HISTORY	V$MANAGED_STANDBY
V$MAP_COMP_LIST	V$MAP_ELEMENT
V$MAP_EXT_ELEMENT	V$MAP_FILE
V$MAP_FILE_EXTENT	V$MAP_FILE_IO_STACK
V$MAP_LIBRARY	V$MAP_SUBELEMENT
V$MAX_ACTIVE_SESS_TARGET_MTH	V$MLS_PARAMETERS
V$MTS	V$MTTR_TARGET_ADVICE
V$MVREFRESH	V$MYSTAT
V$NLS_PARAMETERS	V$NLS_VALID_VALUES
V$OBJECT_DEPENDENCY	V$OBJECT_USAGE
V$OBSOLETE_PARAMETER	V$OFFLINE_RANGE
V$OPEN_CURSOR	V$OPTION
V$PARALLEL_DEGREE_LIMIT_MTH	V$PARAMETER
V$PARAMETER2	V$PGASTAT
V$PGA_TARGET_ADVICE	V$PGA_TARGET_ADVICE_HISTOGRAM

Table 3-2 Complete List of "V$" Synonyms (continued)

V$PQ_SESSTAT	V$PQ_SLAVE
V$PQ_SYSSTAT	V$PQ_TQSTAT
V$PROCESS	V$PROXY_ARCHIVEDLOG
V$PROXY_DATAFILE	V$PWFILE_USERS
V$PX_PROCESS	V$PX_PROCESS_SYSSTAT
V$PX_SESSION	V$PX_SESSTAT
V$QUEUE	V$QUEUEING_MTH
V$RECOVERY_FILE_STATUS	V$RECOVERY_LOG
V$RECOVERY_PROGRESS	V$RECOVERY_STATUS
V$RECOVER_FILE	V$REPLPROP
V$REPLQUEUE	V$REQDIST
V$RESERVED_WORDS	V$RESOURCE
V$RESOURCE_LIMIT	V$RESUMABLE
V$RMAN_CONFIGURATION	V$ROLLNAME
V$ROLLSTAT	V$ROWCACHE
V$ROWCACHE_PARENT	V$ROWCACHE_SUBORDINATE
V$RSRC_CONSUMER_GROUP	V$RSRC_CONSUMER_GROUP_CPU_MTH
V$RSRC_PLAN	V$RSRC_PLAN_CPU_MTH
V$SEGMENT_STATISTICS	V$SEGSTAT
V$SEGSTAT_NAME	V$SESSION
V$SESSION_CONNECT_INFO	V$SESSION_CURSOR_CACHE

Table 3-2   Complete List of "V$" Synonyms (continued)

V$SESSION_EVENT	V$SESSION_LONGOPS
V$SESSION_OBJECT_CACHE	V$SESSION_WAIT
V$SESSTAT	V$SESS_IO
V$SGA	V$SGASTAT
V$SGA_CURRENT_RESIZE_OPS	V$SGA_DYNAMIC_COMPONENTS
V$SGA_DYNAMIC_FREE_MEMORY	V$SGA_RESIZE_OPS
V$SHARED_POOL_ADVICE	V$SHARED_POOL_RESERVED
V$SHARED_SERVER	V$SHARED_SERVER_MONITOR
V$SORT_SEGMENT	V$SORT_USAGE
V$SPPARAMETER	V$SQL
V$SQLAREA	V$SQLTEXT
V$SQLTEXT_WITH_NEWLINES	V$SQLXS
V$SQL_BIND_DATA	V$SQL_BIND_METADATA
V$SQL_CURSOR	V$SQL_PLAN
V$SQL_PLAN_STATISTICS	V$SQL_PLAN_STATISTICS_ALL
V$SQL_REDIRECTION	V$SQL_SHARED_CURSOR
V$SQL_SHARED_MEMORY	V$SQL_WORKAREA
V$SQL_WORKAREA_ACTIVE	V$SQL_WORKAREA_HISTOGRAM
V$STANDBY_LOG	V$STATISTICS_LEVEL
V$STATNAME	V$STREAMS_APPLY_COORDINATOR
V$STREAMS_APPLY_READER	V$STREAMS_APPLY_SERVER

Table 3-2 Complete List of "V$" Synonyms (continued)

V$STREAMS_CAPTURE	V$SUBCACHE
V$SYSSTAT	V$SYSTEM_CURSOR_CACHE
V$SYSTEM_EVENT	V$SYSTEM_PARAMETER
V$SYSTEM_PARAMETER2	V$TABLESPACE
V$TEMPFILE	V$TEMPORARY_LOBS
V$TEMPSEG_USAGE	V$TEMPSTAT
V$TEMPSTATXS	V$TEMP_CACHE_TRANSFER
V$TEMP_EXTENT_MAP	V$TEMP_EXTENT_POOL
V$TEMP_PING	V$TEMP_SPACE_HEADER
V$THREAD	V$TIMER
V$TIMEZONE_NAMES	V$TRANSACTION
V$TRANSACTION_ENQUEUE	V$TYPE_SIZE
V$UNDOSTAT	V$VERSION
V$VPD_POLICY	V$WAITSTAT

Table 3-3   List of Underlying Tables in Dynamic Views

View	Columns
V$OBJECT_USAGE	INDEX_NAME
	TABLE_NAME
	MONITORING
	USED
	START_MONITORING
	END_MONITORING
V_$ACCESS	SID
	OWNER
	OBJECT
	TYPE
V_$ACTIVE_INSTANCES	INST_NUMBER
	INST_NAME
V_$ACTIVE_SESS_POOL_MTH	NAME
V_$AQ	QID
	WAITING
	READY
	EXPIRED
	TOTAL_WAIT
	AVERAGE_WAIT
V_$AQ1	QID

Table 3-3 List of Underlying Tables in Dynamic Views (continued)

View	Columns
V_$AQ1 (cont.)	WAITING
	READY
	EXPIRED
	TOTAL_CONSUMERS
	TOTAL_WAIT
	AVERAGE_WAIT
V_$ARCHIVE	GROUP#
	THREAD#
	SEQUENCE#
	ISCURRENT
	CURRENT
	FIRST_CHANGE#
V_$ARCHIVED_LOG	RECID
	STAMP
	NAME
	DEST_ID
	THREAD#
	SEQUENCE#
	RESETLOGS_CHANGE#
	RESETLOGS_TIME

Table 3-3   List of Underlying Tables in Dynamic Views (continued)

View	Columns
V_$ARCHIVED_LOG (cont.)	FIRST_CHANGE#
	FIRST_TIME
	NEXT_CHANGE#
	NEXT_TIME
	BLOCKS
	BLOCK_SIZE
	CREATOR
	REGISTRAR
	STANDBY_DEST
	ARCHIVED
	APPLIED
	DELETED
	STATUS
	COMPLETION_TIME
	DICTIONARY_BEGIN
	DICTIONARY_END
	END_OF_REDO
	BACKUP_COUNT
	ARCHIVAL_THREAD#
	ACTIVATION#

Table 3-3 List of Underlying Tables in Dynamic Views (continued)

View	Columns
V_$ARCHIVE_DEST	DEST_ID
	DEST_NAME
	STATUS
	BINDING
	NAME_SPACE
	TARGET
	ARCHIVER
	SCHEDULE
	DESTINATION
	LOG_SEQUENCE
	REOPEN_SECS
	DELAY_MINS
	NET_TIMEOUT
	PROCESS
	REGISTER
	FAIL_DATE
	FAIL_SEQUENCE
	FAIL_BLOCK
	FAILURE_COUNT
	MAX_FAILURE

Table 3-3   List of Underlying Tables in Dynamic Views (continued)

View	Columns
V_$ARCHIVE_DEST (cont.)	ERROR
	ALTERNATE
	DEPENDENCY
	REMOTE_TEMPLATE
	QUOTA_SIZE
	QUOTA_USED
	MOUNTID
	TRANSMIT_MODE
	ASYNC_BLOCKS
	AFFIRM
	TYPE
V_$ARCHIVE_DEST_STATUS	DEST_ID
	DEST_NAME
	STATUS
	TYPE
	DATABASE_MODE
	RECOVERY_MODE
	PROTECTION_MODE
	DESTINATION
	STANDBY_LOGFILE_COUNT

Table 3-3 List of Underlying Tables in Dynamic Views (continued)

View	Columns
V_$ARCHIVE_DEST_STATUS (cont.)	STANDBY_LOGFILE_ACTIVE
	ARCHIVED_THREAD#
	ARCHIVED_SEQ#
	APPLIED_THREAD#
	APPLIED_SEQ#
	ERROR
	SRL
V_$ARCHIVE_GAP	THREAD#
	LOW_SEQUENCE#
	HIGH_SEQUENCE#
V_$ARCHIVE_PROCESSES	PROCESS
	STATUS
	LOG_SEQUENCE
	STATE
V_$AW_CALC	AGGREGATE_CACHE_HITS
	AGGREGATE_CACHE_MISSES
	SESSION_CACHE_HITS
	SESSION_CACHE_MISSES
	POOL_HITS
	POOL_MISSES

Table 3-3   List of Underlying Tables in Dynamic Views (continued)

View	Columns
V_$AW_CALC (cont.)	POOL_NEW_PAGES
	POOL_RECLAIMED_PAGES
	CACHE_WRITES
	POOL_SIZE
V_$AW_OLAP	SESSION_ID
	AW_NUMBER
	ATTACH_MODE
	GENERATION
	TEMP_SPACE_PAGES
	TEMP_SPACE_READS
	LOB_READS
	POOL_CHANGED_PAGES
	POOL_UNCHANGED_PAGES
V_$AW_SESSION_INFO	CLIENT_TYPE
	SESSION_STATE
	SESSION_HANDLE
	USERID
	CURR_DML_COMMAND
	PREV_DML_COMMAND
	TOTAL_TRANSACTION

Table 3-3 List of Underlying Tables in Dynamic Views (continued)

View	Columns
V_$AW_SESSION_INFO (cont.)	TOTAL_TRANSACTION_TIME
	AVERAGE_TRANSACTION_TIME
	TRANSACTION_CPU_TIME
	TOTAL_TRANSACTION_CPU_TIME
	AVERAGE_TRANSACTION_CPU_TIME
V_$BACKUP	FILE#
	STATUS
	CHANGE#
	TIME
V_$BACKUP_ASYNC_IO	SID
	SERIAL
	USE_COUNT
	DEVICE_TYPE
	TYPE
	STATUS
	FILENAME
	SET_COUNT
	SET_STAMP
	BUFFER_SIZE
	BUFFER_COUNT

Table 3-3 List of Underlying Tables in Dynamic Views (continued)

View	Columns
V_$BACKUP_ASYNC_IO (cont.)	TOTAL_BYTES
	OPEN_TIME
	CLOSE_TIME
	ELAPSED_TIME
	MAXOPENFILES
	BYTES
	EFFECTIVE_BYTES_PER_SECOND
	IO_COUNT
	READY
	SHORT_WAITS
	SHORT_WAIT_TIME_TOTAL
	SHORT_WAIT_TIME_MAX
	LONG_WAITS
	LONG_WAIT_TIME_TOTAL
	LONG_WAIT_TIME_MAX
V_$BACKUP_CORRUPTION	RECID
	STAMP
	SET_STAMP
	SET_COUNT
	PIECE#

Table 3-3 List of Underlying Tables in Dynamic Views (continued)

View	Columns
V_$BACKUP_CORRUPTION (cont.)	FILE#
	BLOCK#
	BLOCKS
	CORRUPTION_CHANGE#
	MARKED_CORRUPT
	CORRUPTION_TYPE
V_$BACKUP_DATAFILE	RECID
	STAMP
	SET_STAMP
	SET_COUNT
	FILE#
	CREATION_CHANGE#
	CREATION_TIME
	RESETLOGS_CHANGE#
	RESETLOGS_TIME
	INCREMENTAL_LEVEL
	INCREMENTAL_CHANGE#
	CHECKPOINT_CHANGE#
	CHECKPOINT_TIME
	ABSOLUTE_FUZZY_CHANGE#

Table 3-3   List of Underlying Tables in Dynamic Views (continued)

View	Columns
V_$BACKUP_DATAFILE (cont.)	MARKED_CORRUPT
	MEDIA_CORRUPT
	LOGICALLY_CORRUPT
	DATAFILE_BLOCKS
	BLOCKS
	BLOCK_SIZE
	OLDEST_OFFLINE_RANGE
	COMPLETION_TIME
	CONTROLFILE_TYPE
V_$BACKUP_DEVICE	DEVICE_TYPE
	DEVICE_NAME
V_$BACKUP_PIECE	RECID
	STAMP
	SET_STAMP
	SET_COUNT
	PIECE#
	COPY#
	DEVICE_TYPE
	HANDLE
	COMMENTS

Table 3-3 List of Underlying Tables in Dynamic Views *(continued)*

View	Columns
V_$BACKUP_PIECE (cont.)	MEDIA
	MEDIA_POOL
	CONCUR
	TAG
	STATUS
	START_TIME
	COMPLETION_TIME
	ELAPSED_SECONDS
	DELETED
V_$BACKUP_REDOLOG	RECID
	STAMP
	SET_STAMP
	SET_COUNT
	THREAD#
	SEQUENCE#
	RESETLOGS_CHANGE#
	RESETLOGS_TIME
	FIRST_CHANGE#
	FIRST_TIME
	NEXT_CHANGE#

Table 3-3   List of Underlying Tables in Dynamic Views (continued)

View	Columns
V_$BACKUP_REDOLOG (cont.)	NEXT_TIME
	BLOCKS
	BLOCK_SIZE
V_$BACKUP_SET	RECID
	STAMP
	SET_STAMP
	SET_COUNT
	BACKUP_TYPE
	CONTROLFILE_INCLUDED
	INCREMENTAL_LEVEL
	PIECES
	START_TIME
	COMPLETION_TIME
	ELAPSED_SECONDS
	BLOCK_SIZE
	INPUT_FILE_SCAN_ONLY
	KEEP
	KEEP_UNTIL
	KEEP_OPTIONS
V_$BACKUP_SPFILE	RECID

Table 3-3 List of Underlying Tables in Dynamic Views *(continued)*

View	Columns
V_$BACKUP_SPFILE (cont.)	STAMP
	SET_STAMP
	SET_COUNT
	MODIFICATION_TIME
	BYTES
	COMPLETION_TIME
V_$BACKUP_SYNC_IO	SID
	SERIAL
	USE_COUNT
	DEVICE_TYPE
	TYPE
	STATUS
	FILENAME
	SET_COUNT
	SET_STAMP
	BUFFER_SIZE
	BUFFER_COUNT
	TOTAL_BYTES
	OPEN_TIME
	CLOSE_TIME

Table 3-3 List of Underlying Tables in Dynamic Views (continued)

View	Columns
V_$BACKUP_SYNC_IO (cont.)	ELAPSED_TIME
	MAXOPENFILES
	BYTES
	EFFECTIVE_BYTES_PER_SECOND
	IO_COUNT
	IO_TIME_TOTAL
	IO_TIME_MAX
	DISCRETE_BYTES_PER_SECOND
V_$BGPROCESS	PADDR
	NAME
	DESCRIPTION
	ERROR
V_$BH	FILE#
	BLOCK#
	CLASS#
	STATUS
	XNC
	FORCED_READS
	FORCED_WRITES
	LOCK_ELEMENT_ADDR

Table 3-3 List of Underlying Tables in Dynamic Views (continued)

View	Columns
V_$BH (cont.)	LOCK_ELEMENT_NAME
	LOCK_ELEMENT_CLASS
	DIRTY
	TEMP
	PING
	STALE
	DIRECT
	NEW
	OBJD
	TS#
V_$BSP	CR_REQUESTS
	CURRENT_REQUESTS
	DATA_REQUESTS
	UNDO_REQUESTS
	TX_REQUESTS
	CURRENT_RESULTS
	PRIVATE_RESULTS
	ZERO_RESULTS
	DISK_READ_RESULTS
	FAIL_RESULTS

Table 3-3   List of Underlying Tables in Dynamic Views (continued)

View	Columns
V_$BSP (cont.)	FAIRNESS_DOWN_CONVERTS
	FAIRNESS_CLEARS
	FREE_LOCK_ELEMENTS
	FLUSHES
	FLUSHES_QUEUED
	FLUSH_QUEUE_FULL
	FLUSH_MAX_TIME
	LIGHT_WORKS
	ERRORS
V_$BUFFER_POOL	BUFFERS
	TARGET_SIZE
	TARGET_BUFFERS
	PREV_SIZE
	PREV_BUFFERS
	LO_BNUM
	HI_BNUM
	LO_SETID
	HI_SETID
	SET_COUNT
	ID

Table 3-3 List of Underlying Tables in Dynamic Views (continued)

View	Columns
V_$BUFFER_POOL (cont.)	NAME
	BLOCK_SIZE
	RESIZE_STATE
	CURRENT_SIZE
V_$BUFFER_POOL_STATISTICS	ID
	NAME
	BLOCK_SIZE
	SET_MSIZE
	CNUM_REPL
	CNUM_WRITE
	CNUM_SET
	BUF_GOT
	SUM_WRITE
	SUM_SCAN
	FREE_BUFFER_WAIT
	WRITE_COMPLETE_WAIT
	BUFFER_BUSY_WAIT
	FREE_BUFFER_INSPECTED
	DIRTY_BUFFERS_INSPECTED
	DB_BLOCK_CHANGE

Table 3-3 List of Underlying Tables in Dynamic Views (continued)

View	Columns
V_$BUFFER_POOL_STATISTICS (cont.)	DB_BLOCK_GETS
	CONSISTENT_GETS
	PHYSICAL_READS
	PHYSICAL_WRITES
V_$CIRCUIT	CIRCUIT
	DISPATCHER
	SERVER
	WAITER
	SADDR
	STATUS
	QUEUE
	MESSAGE0
	MESSAGE1
	MESSAGE2
	MESSAGE3
	MESSAGES
	BYTES
	BREAKS
	PRESENTATION
	PCIRCUIT

Table 3-3 List of Underlying Tables in Dynamic Views (continued)

View	Columns
V_$CLASS_CACHE_TRANSFER	CLASS
	X_2_NULL
	X_2_NULL_FORCED_WRITE
	X_2_NULL_FORCED_STALE
	X_2_S
	X_2_S_FORCED_WRITE
	S_2_NULL
	S_2_NULL_FORCED_STALE
	NULL_2_X
	S_2_X
	NULL_2_S
V_$CLASS_PING	CLASS
	X_2_NULL
	X_2_NULL_FORCED_WRITE
	X_2_NULL_FORCED_STALE
	X_2_S
	X_2_S_FORCED_WRITE
	X_2_SSX
	X_2_SSX_FORCED_WRITE
	S_2_NULL

Table 3-3   List of Underlying Tables in Dynamic Views (continued)

View	Columns
V_$CLASS_PING (cont.)	S_2_NULL_FORCED_STALE
	SS_2_NULL
	SS_2_RLS
	OP_2_SS
	NULL_2_X
	S_2_X
	SSX_2_X
	NULL_2_S
	NULL_2_SS
V_$COMPATIBILITY	TYPE_ID
	RELEASE
	DESCRIPTION
V_$COMPATSEG	TYPE_ID
	RELEASE
	UPDATED
V_$CONTEXT	NAMESPACE
	ATTRIBUTE
	VALUE
V_$CONTROLFILE	STATUS
	NAME

Table 3-3 List of Underlying Tables in Dynamic Views (continued)

View	Columns
V_$CONTROLFILE_RECORD_SECTION	TYPE
	RECORD_SIZE
	RECORDS_TOTAL
	RECORDS_USED
	FIRST_INDEX
	LAST_INDEX
	LAST_RECID
V_$COPY_CORRUPTION	RECID
	STAMP
	COPY_RECID
	COPY_STAMP
	FILE#
	BLOCK#
	BLOCKS
	CORRUPTION_CHANGE#
	MARKED_CORRUPT
	CORRUPTION_TYPE
V_$CR_BLOCK_SERVER	CR_REQUESTS
	CURRENT_REQUESTS
	DATA_REQUESTS

Table 3-3 List of Underlying Tables in Dynamic Views (continued)

View	Columns
V_$CR_BLOCK_SERVER (cont.)	UNDO_REQUESTS
	TX_REQUESTS
	CURRENT_RESULTS
	PRIVATE_RESULTS
	ZERO_RESULTS
	DISK_READ_RESULTS
	FAIL_RESULTS
	FAIRNESS_DOWN_CONVERTS
	FAIRNESS_CLEARS
	FREE_GC_ELEMENTS
	FLUSHES
	FLUSHES_QUEUED
	FLUSH_QUEUE_FULL
	FLUSH_MAX_TIME
	LIGHT_WORKS
	ERRORS
V_$DATABASE	DBID
	NAME
	CREATED
	RESETLOGS_CHANGE#

Table 3-3   List of Underlying Tables in Dynamic Views (continued)

View	Columns
V_$DATABASE (cont.)	RESETLOGS_TIME
	PRIOR_RESETLOGS_CHANGE#
	PRIOR_RESETLOGS_TIME
	LOG_MODE
	CHECKPOINT_CHANGE#
	ARCHIVE_CHANGE#
	CONTROLFILE_TYPE
	CONTROLFILE_CREATED
	CONTROLFILE_SEQUENCE#
	CONTROLFILE_CHANGE#
	CONTROLFILE_TIME
	OPEN_RESETLOGS
	VERSION_TIME
	OPEN_MODE
	PROTECTION_MODE
	PROTECTION_LEVEL
	REMOTE_ARCHIVE
	ACTIVATION#
	DATABASE_ROLE
	ARCHIVELOG_CHANGE#

Table 3-3   List of Underlying Tables in Dynamic Views (continued)

View	Columns
V_$DATABASE (cont.)	SWITCHOVER_STATUS
	DATAGUARD_BROKER
	GUARD_STATUS
	SUPPLEMENTAL_LOG_DATA_MIN
	SUPPLEMENTAL_LOG_DATA_PK
	SUPPLEMENTAL_LOG_DATA_UI
	FORCE_LOGGING
V_$DATABASE_BLOCK_CORRUPTION	FILE#
	BLOCK#
	BLOCKS
	CORRUPTION_CHANGE#
	CORRUPTION_TYPE
V_$DATABASE_INCARNATION	RESETLOGS_CHANGE#
	RESETLOGS_TIME
	PRIOR_RESETLOGS_CHANGE#
	PRIOR_RESETLOGS_TIME
V_$DATAFILE	FILE#
	CREATION_CHANGE#
	CREATION_TIME
	TS#

Table 3-3 List of Underlying Tables in Dynamic Views (continued)

View	Columns
V_$DATAFILE (cont.)	RFILE#
	STATUS
	ENABLED
	CHECKPOINT_CHANGE#
	CHECKPOINT_TIME
	UNRECOVERABLE_CHANGE#
	UNRECOVERABLE_TIME
	LAST_CHANGE#
	LAST_TIME
	OFFLINE_CHANGE#
	ONLINE_CHANGE#
	ONLINE_TIME
	BYTES
	BLOCKS
	CREATE_BYTES
	BLOCK_SIZE
	NAME
	PLUGGED_IN
	BLOCK1_OFFSET
	AUX_NAME

Table 3-3 List of Underlying Tables in Dynamic Views (continued)

View	Columns
V_$DATAFILE_COPY	TAG
	FILE#
	RFILE#
	CREATION_CHANGE#
	CREATION_TIME
	RESETLOGS_CHANGE#
	RESETLOGS_TIME
	INCREMENTAL_LEVEL
	CHECKPOINT_CHANGE#
	CHECKPOINT_TIME
	ABSOLUTE_FUZZY_CHANGE#
	RECOVERY_FUZZY_CHANGE#
	RECOVERY_FUZZY_TIME
	ONLINE_FUZZY
	BACKUP_FUZZY
	MARKED_CORRUPT
	MEDIA_CORRUPT
	LOGICALLY_CORRUPT
	BLOCKS
	BLOCK_SIZE

Table 3-3 List of Underlying Tables in Dynamic Views (continued)

View	Columns
V_$DATAFILE_COPY (cont.)	OLDEST_OFFLINE_RANGE
	DELETED
	STATUS
	COMPLETION_TIME
	CONTROLFILE_TYPE
	KEEP
	KEEP_UNTIL
	KEEP_OPTIONS
	SCANNED
	RECID
	STAMP
	NAME
V_$DATAFILE_HEADER	FILE#
	STATUS
	ERROR
	FORMAT
	RECOVER
	FUZZY
	CREATION_CHANGE#
	CREATION_TIME

Table 3-3 List of Underlying Tables in Dynamic Views (continued)

View	Columns
V_$DATAFILE_HEADER (cont.)	TABLESPACE_NAME
	TS#
	RFILE#
	RESETLOGS_CHANGE#
	RESETLOGS_TIME
	CHECKPOINT_CHANGE#
	CHECKPOINT_TIME
	CHECKPOINT_COUNT
	BYTES
	BLOCKS
	NAME
V_$DATAGUARD_STATUS	FACILITY
	SEVERITY
	DEST_ID
	MESSAGE_NUM
	ERROR_CODE
	CALLOUT
	TIMESTAMP
	MESSAGE
V_$DBFILE	FILE#

Table 3-3   List of Underlying Tables in Dynamic Views (continued)

View	Columns
V_$DBFILE (cont.)	NAME
V_$DBLINK	DB_LINK
	OWNER_ID
	LOGGED_ON
	HETEROGENEOUS
	PROTOCOL
	OPEN_CURSORS
	IN_TRANSACTION
	UPDATE_SENT
	COMMIT_POINT_STRENGTH
V_$DB_CACHE_ADVICE	ID
	NAME
	BLOCK_SIZE
	ADVICE_STATUS
	SIZE_FOR_ESTIMATE
	SIZE_FACTOR
	BUFFERS_FOR_ESTIMATE
	ESTD_PHYSICAL_READ_FACTOR
	ESTD_PHYSICAL_READS
V_$DB_OBJECT_CACHE	OWNER

Table 3-3   List of Underlying Tables in Dynamic Views (continued)

View	Columns
V_$DB_OBJECT_CACHE (cont.)	NAME
	DB_LINK
	NAMESPACE
	TYPE
	SHARABLE_MEM
	LOADS
	EXECUTIONS
	LOCKS
	PINS
	KEPT
	CHILD_LATCH
V_$DB_PIPES	OWNERID
	NAME
	TYPE
	PIPE_SIZE
V_$DELETED_OBJECT	RECID
	STAMP
	TYPE
	OBJECT_RECID
	OBJECT_STAMP

Table 3-3 List of Underlying Tables in Dynamic Views (continued)

View	Columns
V_$DELETED_OBJECT (cont.)	OBJECT_DATA
V_$DISPATCHER	NAME
	NETWORK
	PADDR
	STATUS
	ACCEPT
	MESSAGES
	BYTES
	BREAKS
	OWNED
	CREATED
	IDLE
	BUSY
	LISTENER
	CONF_INDX
V_$DISPATCHER_RATE	AVG_EVENT_RATE
	AVG_EVENTS_PER_LOOP
	AVG_MSG_RATE
	AVG_SVR_BUF_RATE
	AVG_SVR_BYTE_RATE

Table 3-3 List of Underlying Tables in Dynamic Views (continued)

View	Columns
V_$DISPATCHER_RATE (cont.)	AVG_SVR_BYTE_PER_BUF
	AVG_CLT_BUF_RATE
	AVG_CLT_BYTE_RATE
	AVG_CLT_BYTE_PER_BUF
	AVG_BUF_RATE
	AVG_BYTE_RATE
	AVG_BYTE_PER_BUF
	AVG_IN_CONNECT_RATE
	AVG_OUT_CONNECT_RATE
	AVG_RECONNECT_RATE
	TTL_LOOPS
	TTL_MSG
	TTL_SVR_BUF
	TTL_CLT_BUF
	TTL_BUF
	TTL_IN_CONNECT
	TTL_OUT_CONNECT
	TTL_RECONNECT
	SCALE_LOOPS
	SCALE_MSG

Table 3-3 List of Underlying Tables in Dynamic Views *(continued)*

View	Columns
V_$DISPATCHER_RATE (cont.)	SCALE_SVR_BUF
	SCALE_CLT_BUF
	SCALE_BUF
	SCALE_IN_CONNECT
	SCALE_OUT_CONNECT
	SCALE_RECONNECT
	NAME
	PADDR
	CUR_LOOP_RATE
	CUR_EVENT_RATE
	CUR_EVENTS_PER_LOOP
	CUR_MSG_RATE
	CUR_SVR_BUF_RATE
	CUR_SVR_BYTE_RATE
	CUR_SVR_BYTE_PER_BUF
	CUR_CLT_BUF_RATE
	CUR_CLT_BYTE_RATE
	CUR_CLT_BYTE_PER_BUF
	CUR_BUF_RATE
	CUR_BYTE_RATE

Table 3-3 List of Underlying Tables in Dynamic Views (continued)

View	Columns
V_$DISPATCHER_RATE (cont.)	CUR_BYTE_PER_BUF
	CUR_IN_CONNECT_RATE
	CUR_OUT_CONNECT_RATE
	CUR_RECONNECT_RATE
	MAX_LOOP_RATE
	MAX_EVENT_RATE
	MAX_EVENTS_PER_LOOP
	MAX_MSG_RATE
	MAX_SVR_BUF_RATE
	MAX_SVR_BYTE_RATE
	MAX_SVR_BYTE_PER_BUF
	MAX_CLT_BUF_RATE
	MAX_CLT_BYTE_RATE
	MAX_CLT_BYTE_PER_BUF
	MAX_BUF_RATE
	MAX_BYTE_RATE
	MAX_BYTE_PER_BUF
	MAX_IN_CONNECT_RATE
	MAX_OUT_CONNECT_RATE
	MAX_RECONNECT_RATE

Table 3-3 List of Underlying Tables in Dynamic Views (continued)

View	Columns
V_$DISPATCHER_RATE (cont.)	AVG_LOOP_RATE
V_$DLM_ALL_LOCKS	LOCKP
	GRANT_LEVEL
	REQUEST_LEVEL
	RESOURCE_NAME1
	RESOURCE_NAME2
	PID
	TRANSACTION_ID0
	TRANSACTION_ID1
	GROUP_ID
	OPEN_OPT_DEADLOCK
	OPEN_OPT_PERSISTENT
	OPEN_OPT_PROCESS_OWNED
	OPEN_OPT_NO_XID
	CONVERT_OPT_GETVALUE
	CONVERT_OPT_PUTVALUE
	CONVERT_OPT_NOVALUE
	CONVERT_OPT_DUBVALUE
	CONVERT_OPT_NOQUEUE
	CONVERT_OPT_EXPRESS

Table 3-3   List of Underlying Tables in Dynamic Views (continued)

View	Columns
V_$DLM_ALL_LOCKS (cont.)	CONVERT_OPT_NODEADLOCKWAIT
	CONVERT_OPT_NODEADLOCKBLOCK
	WHICH_QUEUE
	LOCKSTATE
	AST_EVENT0
	OWNER_NODE
	BLOCKED
	BLOCKER
V_$DLM_CONVERT_LOCAL	INST_ID
	CONVERT_TYPE
	AVERAGE_CONVERT_TIME
	CONVERT_COUNT
V_$DLM_CONVERT_REMOTE	INST_ID
	CONVERT_TYPE
	AVERAGE_CONVERT_TIME
	CONVERT_COUNT
V_$DLM_LATCH	IMMEDIATE_GETS
	IMMEDIATE_MISSES
	WAITERS_WOKEN
	WAITS_HOLDING_LATCH

Table 3-3 List of Underlying Tables in Dynamic Views (continued)

View	Columns
V_$DLM_LATCH (cont.)	SPIN_GETS
	SLEEP1
	SLEEP2
	SLEEP3
	SLEEP4
	SLEEP5
	SLEEP6
	SLEEP7
	SLEEP8
	SLEEP9
	SLEEP10
	SLEEP11
	WAIT_TIME
	ADDR
	LATCH#
	LEVEL#
	NAME
	GETS
	MISSES
	SLEEPS

Table 3-3 List of Underlying Tables in Dynamic Views (continued)

View	Columns
V_$DLM_LOCKS	LOCKP
	GRANT_LEVEL
	REQUEST_LEVEL
	RESOURCE_NAME1
	RESOURCE_NAME2
	PID
	TRANSACTION_ID0
	TRANSACTION_ID1
	GROUP_ID
	OPEN_OPT_DEADLOCK
	OPEN_OPT_PERSISTENT
	OPEN_OPT_PROCESS_OWNED
	OPEN_OPT_NO_XID
	CONVERT_OPT_GETVALUE
	CONVERT_OPT_PUTVALUE
	CONVERT_OPT_NOVALUE
	CONVERT_OPT_DUBVALUE
	CONVERT_OPT_NOQUEUE
	CONVERT_OPT_EXPRESS
	CONVERT_OPT_NODEADLOCKWAIT

Table 3-3 List of Underlying Tables in Dynamic Views (continued)

View	Columns
V_$DLM_LOCKS (cont.)	CONVERT_OPT_NODEADLOCKBLOCK
	WHICH_QUEUE
	LOCKSTATE
	AST_EVENT0
	OWNER_NODE
	BLOCKED
	BLOCKER
V_$DLM_MISC	STATISTIC#
	NAME
	VALUE
V_$DLM_RESS	RESP
	RESOURCE_NAME
	ON_CONVERT_Q
	ON_GRANT_Q
	PERSISTENT_RES
	MASTER_NODE
	NEXT_CVT_LEVEL
	VALUE_BLK_STATE
	VALUE_BLK
V_$DLM_TRAFFIC_CONTROLLER	LOCAL_NID

Table 3-3 List of Underlying Tables in Dynamic Views (continued)

View	Columns
V_$DLM_TRAFFIC_CONTROLLER (cont.)	REMOTE_NID
	REMOTE_RID
	REMOTE_INC
	TCKT_AVAIL
	TCKT_LIMIT
	TCKT_RCVD
	TCKT_WAIT
	SND_SEQ_NO
	RCV_SEQ_NO
	SND_Q_LEN
	SND_Q_MAX
	SND_Q_TOT
	SND_Q_TM_BASE
	SND_Q_TM_WRAP
	STATUS
	SND_PROXY
V_$ENABLEDPRIVS	PRIV_NUMBER
V_$ENQUEUE_LOCK	ADDR
	KADDR
	SID

Table 3-3 List of Underlying Tables in Dynamic Views (continued)

View	Columns
V_$ENQUEUE_LOCK (cont.)	TYPE
	ID1
	ID2
	LMODE
	REQUEST
	CTIME
	BLOCK
V_$ENQUEUE_STAT	INST_ID
	EQ_TYPE
	TOTAL_REQ#
	TOTAL_WAIT#
	SUCC_REQ#
	FAILED_REQ#
	CUM_WAIT_TIME
V_$EVENT_NAME	EVENT#
	NAME
	PARAMETER1
	PARAMETER2
	PARAMETER3
V_$EXECUTION	PID

Table 3-3   List of Underlying Tables in Dynamic Views (continued)

View	Columns
V_$EXECUTION (cont.)	DEPTH
	FUNCTION
	TYPE
	NVALS
	VAL1
	VAL2
	SEQH
	SEQL
V_$FAST_START_SERVERS	STATE
	UNDOBLOCKSDONE
	PID
V_$FAST_START_TRANSACTIONS	USN
	SLT
	SEQ
	STATE
	UNDOBLOCKSDONE
	UNDOBLOCKSTOTAL
	PID
	CPUTIME
	PARENTUSN

Table 3-3 List of Underlying Tables in Dynamic Views (continued)

View	Columns
V_$FAST_START_TRANSACTIONS (cont.)	PARENTSLT
	PARENTSEQ
V_$FILESTAT	FILE#
	PHYRDS
	PHYWRTS
	PHYBLKRD
	PHYBLKWRT
	SINGLEBLKRDS
	READTIM
	WRITETIM
	SINGLEBLKRDTIM
	AVGIOTIM
	LSTIOTIM
	MINIOTIM
	MAXIORTM
	MAXIOWTM
V_$FILESTATXS	TSNAME
	FILENAME
	PHYRDS
	PHYWRTS

Table 3-3   List of Underlying Tables in Dynamic Views (continued)

View	Columns
V_$FILESTATXS (cont.)	READTIM
	WRITETIM
	PHYBLKRD
	PHYBLKWRT
	WAIT_COUNT
	TIME
V_$FILE_CACHE_TRANSFER	FILE_NUMBER
	X_2_NULL
	X_2_NULL_FORCED_WRITE
	X_2_NULL_FORCED_STALE
	X_2_S
	X_2_S_FORCED_WRITE
	S_2_NULL
	S_2_NULL_FORCED_STALE
	RBR
	RBR_FORCED_WRITE
	RBR_FORCED_STALE
	NULL_2_X
	S_2_X
	NULL_2_S

Table 3-3 List of Underlying Tables in Dynamic Views (continued)

View	Columns
V_$FILE_CACHE_TRANSFER (cont.)	CR_TRANSFERS
	CUR_TRANSFERS
V_$FILE_PING	FILE_NUMBER
	FREQUENCY
	X_2_NULL
	X_2_NULL_FORCED_WRITE
	X_2_NULL_FORCED_STALE
	X_2_S
	X_2_S_FORCED_WRITE
	X_2_SSX
	X_2_SSX_FORCED_WRITE
	S_2_NULL
	S_2_NULL_FORCED_STALE
	SS_2_NULL
	SS_2_RLS
	WRB
	WRB_FORCED_WRITE
	RBR
	RBR_FORCED_WRITE
	RBR_FORCED_STALE

Table 3-3 List of Underlying Tables in Dynamic Views (continued)

View	Columns
V_$FILE_PING (cont.)	CBR
	CBR_FORCED_WRITE
	NULL_2_X
	S_2_X
	SSX_2_X
	NULL_2_S
	NULL_2_SS
	OP_2_SS
V_$FIXED_TABLE	NAME
	OBJECT_ID
	TYPE
	TABLE_NUM
V_$FIXED_VIEW_DEFINITION	VIEW_NAME
	VIEW_DEFINITION
V_$GCSHVMASTER_INFO	HV_ID
	CURRENT_MASTER
	PREVIOUS_MASTER
	REMASTER_CNT
V_$GCSPFMASTER_INFO	FILE_ID
	CURRENT_MASTER

Table 3-3 List of Underlying Tables in Dynamic Views *(continued)*

View	Columns
V_$GCSPFMASTER_INFO (cont.)	PREVIOUS_MASTER
	REMASTER_CNT
V_$GC_ELEMENT	GC_ELEMENT_ADDR
	INDX
	CLASS
	GC_ELEMENT_NAME
	MODE_HELD
	BLOCK_COUNT
	RELEASING
	ACQUIRING
	WRITING
	RECOVERING
	LOCAL
	FLAGS
V_$GC_ELEMENTS_WITH_COLLISIONS	GC_ELEMENT_ADDR
V_$GES_BLOCKING_ENQUEUE	HANDLE
	GRANT_LEVEL
	REQUEST_LEVEL
	RESOURCE_NAME1
	RESOURCE_NAME2

Table 3-3   List of Underlying Tables in Dynamic Views (continued)

View	Columns
V_$GES_BLOCKING_ENQUEUE (cont.)	PID
	TRANSACTION_ID0
	TRANSACTION_ID1
	GROUP_ID
	OPEN_OPT_DEADLOCK
	OPEN_OPT_PERSISTENT
	OPEN_OPT_PROCESS_OWNED
	OPEN_OPT_NO_XID
	CONVERT_OPT_GETVALUE
	CONVERT_OPT_PUTVALUE
	CONVERT_OPT_NOVALUE
	CONVERT_OPT_DUBVALUE
	CONVERT_OPT_NOQUEUE
	CONVERT_OPT_EXPRESS
	CONVERT_OPT_NODEADLOCKWAIT
	CONVERT_OPT_NODEADLOCKBLOCK
	WHICH_QUEUE
	STATE
	AST_EVENT0
	OWNER_NODE

Table 3-3 List of Underlying Tables in Dynamic Views (continued)

View	Columns
V_$GES_BLOCKING_ENQUEUE (cont.)	BLOCKED
	BLOCKER
V_$GES_ENQUEUE	HANDLE
	GRANT_LEVEL
	REQUEST_LEVEL
	RESOURCE_NAME1
	RESOURCE_NAME2
	PID
	TRANSACTION_ID0
	TRANSACTION_ID1
	GROUP_ID
	OPEN_OPT_DEADLOCK
	OPEN_OPT_PERSISTENT
	OPEN_OPT_PROCESS_OWNED
	OPEN_OPT_NO_XID
	CONVERT_OPT_GETVALUE
	CONVERT_OPT_PUTVALUE
	CONVERT_OPT_NOVALUE
	CONVERT_OPT_DUBVALUE
	CONVERT_OPT_NOQUEUE

Table 3-3 List of Underlying Tables in Dynamic Views (continued)

View	Columns
V_$GES_ENQUEUE (cont.)	CONVERT_OPT_EXPRESS
	CONVERT_OPT_NODEADLOCKWAIT
	CONVERT_OPT_NODEADLOCKBLOCK
	WHICH_QUEUE
	STATE
	AST_EVENT0
	OWNER_NODE
	BLOCKED
	BLOCKER
V_$GLOBALCONTEXT	NAMESPACE
	ATTRIBUTE
	VALUE
	USERNAME
	CLIENT_IDENTIFIER
V_$GLOBAL_BLOCKED_LOCKS	ADDR
	KADDR
	SID
	TYPE
	ID1
	ID2

Table 3-3 List of Underlying Tables in Dynamic Views (continued)

View	Columns
V_$GLOBAL_BLOCKED_LOCKS (cont.)	LMODE
	REQUEST
	CTIME
V_$GLOBAL_TRANSACTION	FORMATID
	GLOBALID
	BRANCHID
	BRANCHES
	REFCOUNT
	PREPARECOUNT
	STATE
	FLAGS
	COUPLING
V_$HS_AGENT	AGENT_ID
	MACHINE
	PROCESS
	PROGRAM
	OSUSER
	STARTTIME
	AGENT_TYPE
	FDS_CLASS_ID

Table 3-3   List of Underlying Tables in Dynamic Views (continued)

View	Columns
V_$HS_AGENT (cont.)	FDS_INST_ID
V_$HS_PARAMETER	HS_SESSION_ID
	PARAMETER
	VALUE
	SOURCE
	ENV
V_$HS_SESSION	HS_SESSION_ID
	AGENT_ID
	SID
	DB_LINK
	DB_LINK_OWNER
	STARTTIME
V_$HVMASTER_INFO	HV_ID
	CURRENT_MASTER
	PREVIOUS_MASTER
	REMASTER_CNT
V_$INDEXED_FIXED_COLUMN	TABLE_NAME
	INDEX_NUMBER
	COLUMN_NAME
	COLUMN_POSITION

Table 3-3 List of Underlying Tables in Dynamic Views (continued)

View	Columns
V_$INSTANCE	INSTANCE_NUMBER
	INSTANCE_NAME
	HOST_NAME
	VERSION
	STARTUP_TIME
	STATUS
	PARALLEL
	THREAD#
	ARCHIVER
	LOG_SWITCH_WAIT
	LOGINS
	SHUTDOWN_PENDING
	DATABASE_STATUS
	INSTANCE_ROLE
	ACTIVE_STATE
V_$INSTANCE_RECOVERY	RECOVERY_ESTIMATED_IOS
	ACTUAL_REDO_BLKS
	TARGET_REDO_BLKS
	LOG_FILE_SIZE_REDO_BLKS
	LOG_CHKPT_TIMEOUT_REDO_BLKS

Table 3-3 List of Underlying Tables in Dynamic Views (continued)

View	Columns
V_$INSTANCE_RECOVERY (cont.)	LOG_CHKPT_INTERVAL_REDO_BLKS
	FAST_START_IO_TARGET_REDO_BLKS
	TARGET_MTTR
	ESTIMATED_MTTR
	CKPT_BLOCK_WRITES
V_$LATCH	ADDR
	LATCH#
	LEVEL#
	NAME
	GETS
	MISSES
	SLEEPS
	IMMEDIATE_GETS
	IMMEDIATE_MISSES
	WAITERS_WOKEN
	WAITS_HOLDING_LATCH
	SPIN_GETS
	SLEEP1
	SLEEP2
	SLEEP3

Table 3-3 List of Underlying Tables in Dynamic Views (continued)

View	Columns
V_$LATCH (cont.)	SLEEP4
	SLEEP5
	SLEEP6
	SLEEP7
	SLEEP8
	SLEEP9
	SLEEP10
	SLEEP11
	WAIT_TIME
V_$LATCHHOLDER	PID
	SID
	LADDR
	NAME
V_$LATCHNAME	LATCH#
	NAME
V_$LATCH_CHILDREN	ADDR
	LATCH#
	CHILD#
	LEVEL#
	NAME

Table 3-3   List of Underlying Tables in Dynamic Views (continued)

View	Columns
V_$LATCH_CHILDREN (cont.)	GETS
	MISSES
	SLEEPS
	IMMEDIATE_GETS
	IMMEDIATE_MISSES
	WAITERS_WOKEN
	WAITS_HOLDING_LATCH
	SPIN_GETS
	SLEEP1
	SLEEP2
	SLEEP3
	SLEEP4
	SLEEP5
	SLEEP6
	SLEEP7
	SLEEP8
	SLEEP9
	SLEEP10
	SLEEP11
	WAIT_TIME

Table 3-3 List of Underlying Tables in Dynamic Views (continued)

View	Columns
V_$LATCH_MISSES	PARENT_NAME
	WHERE
	NWFAIL_COUNT
	SLEEP_COUNT
	WTR_SLP_COUNT
	LONGHOLD_COUNT
	LOCATION
V_$LATCH_PARENT	ADDR
	LATCH#
	LEVEL#
	NAME
	GETS
	MISSES
	SLEEPS
	IMMEDIATE_GETS
	IMMEDIATE_MISSES
	WAITERS_WOKEN
	WAITS_HOLDING_LATCH
	SPIN_GETS
	SLEEP1

Table 3-3   List of Underlying Tables in Dynamic Views (continued)

View	Columns
V_$LATCH_PARENT (cont.)	SLEEP2
	SLEEP3
	SLEEP4
	SLEEP5
	SLEEP6
	SLEEP7
	SLEEP8
	SLEEP9
	SLEEP10
	SLEEP11
	WAIT_TIME
V_$LIBRARYCACHE	NAMESPACE
	GETS
	GETHITS
	GETHITRATIO
	PINS
	PINHITS
	PINHITRATIO
	RELOADS
	INVALIDATIONS

Table 3-3   List of Underlying Tables in Dynamic Views (continued)

View	Columns
V_$LIBRARYCACHE (cont.)	DLM_LOCK_REQUESTS
	DLM_PIN_REQUESTS
	DLM_PIN_RELEASES
	DLM_INVALIDATION_REQUESTS
	DLM_INVALIDATIONS
V_$LIBRARY_CACHE_MEMORY	LC_NAMESPACE
	LC_INUSE_MEMORY_OBJECTS
	LC_INUSE_MEMORY_SIZE
	LC_FREEABLE_MEMORY_OBJECTS
	LC_FREEABLE_MEMORY_SIZE
V_$LICENSE	SESSIONS_MAX
	SESSIONS_WARNING
	SESSIONS_CURRENT
	SESSIONS_HIGHWATER
	USERS_MAX
V_$LOADISTAT	OWNER
	TABNAME
	INDEXNAME
	SUBNAME
	MESSAGE

Table 3-3   List of Underlying Tables in Dynamic Views (continued)

View	Columns
V_$LOADPSTAT	OWNER
	TABNAME
	PARTNAME
	LOADED
V_$LOCK	ADDR
	KADDR
	SID
	TYPE
	ID1
	ID2
	LMODE
	REQUEST
	CTIME
	BLOCK
V_$LOCKED_OBJECT	ORACLE_USERNAME
	OS_USER_NAME
	PROCESS
	LOCKED_MODE
	XIDUSN
	XIDSLOT

Table 3-3 List of Underlying Tables in Dynamic Views (continued)

View	Columns
V_$LOCKED_OBJECT (cont.)	XIDSQN
	OBJECT_ID
	SESSION_ID
V_$LOCKS_WITH_COLLISIONS	LOCK_ELEMENT_ADDR
V_$LOCK_ACTIVITY	TO_VAL
	ACTION_VAL
	COUNTER
	FROM_VAL
V_$LOCK_ELEMENT	LOCK_ELEMENT_ADDR
	INDX
	CLASS
	LOCK_ELEMENT_NAME
	MODE_HELD
	BLOCK_COUNT
	RELEASING
	ACQUIRING
	INVALID
	FLAGS
V_$LOG	GROUP#
	THREAD#

Table 3-3   List of Underlying Tables in Dynamic Views (continued)

View	Columns
V_$LOG (cont.)	SEQUENCE#
	BYTES
	MEMBERS
	ARCHIVED
	STATUS
	FIRST_CHANGE#
	FIRST_TIME
V_$LOGFILE	GROUP#
	STATUS
	TYPE
	MEMBER
V_$LOGHIST	THREAD#
	SEQUENCE#
	FIRST_CHANGE#
	FIRST_TIME
	SWITCH_CHANGE#
V_$LOGMNR_CALLBACK	STATE
	TYPE
	CAPABILITY
V_$LOGMNR_CONTENTS	SCN

Table 3-3 List of Underlying Tables in Dynamic Views (continued)

View	Columns
V_$LOGMNR_CONTENTS (cont.)	CSCN
	TIMESTAMP
	COMMIT_TIMESTAMP
	THREAD#
	LOG_ID
	XIDUSN
	XIDSLT
	XIDSQN
	PXIDUSN
	PXIDSLT
	PXIDSQN
	RBASQN
	RBABLK
	RBABYTE
	UBAFIL
	UBABLK
	UBAREC
	UBASQN
	ABS_FILE#
	REL_FILE#

Table 3-3   List of Underlying Tables in Dynamic Views (continued)

View	Columns
V_$LOGMNR_CONTENTS (cont.)	DATA_BLK#
	DATA_OBJ#
	DATA_OBJD#
	SEG_OWNER
	SEG_NAME
	SEG_TYPE
	SEG_TYPE_NAME
	TABLE_SPACE
	ROW_ID
	SESSION#
	SERIAL#
	USERNAME
	SESSION_INFO
	TX_NAME
	ROLLBACK
	OPERATION
	OPERATION_CODE
	SQL_REDO
	SQL_UNDO
	RS_ID

Table 3-3 List of Underlying Tables in Dynamic Views (continued)

View	Columns
V_$LOGMNR_CONTENTS (cont.)	SEQUENCE#
	SSN
	CSF
	INFO
	STATUS
	REDO_VALUE
	UNDO_VALUE
	SQL_COLUMN_TYPE
	SQL_COLUMN_NAME
	REDO_LENGTH
	REDO_OFFSET
	UNDO_LENGTH
	UNDO_OFFSET
V_$LOGMNR_DICTIONARY	TIMESTAMP
	DB_ID
	DB_NAME
	FILENAME
	DICTIONARY_SCN
	RESET_SCN
	RESET_SCN_TIME

Table 3-3 List of Underlying Tables in Dynamic Views (continued)

View	Columns
V_$LOGMNR_DICTIONARY (cont.)	ENABLED_THREAD_MAP
	INFO
	STATUS
V_$LOGMNR_LOGFILE	LOG_ID
	FILENAME
	LOW_TIME
	NEXT_TIME
	DB_ID
	DB_NAME
	RESET_SCNWRP
	RESET_SCNBAS
	RESET_SCN_TIME
	THREAD_ID
	THREAD_SQN
	LOW_SCNWRP
	LOW_SCNBAS
	NEXT_SCNWRP
	NEXT_SCNBAS
	FILE_STATE
V_$LOGMNR_LOGS	LOG_ID

Table 3-3   List of Underlying Tables in Dynamic Views (continued)

View	Columns
V_$LOGMNR_LOGS (cont.)	FILENAME
	LOW_TIME
	HIGH_TIME
	DB_ID
	DB_NAME
	RESET_SCN
	RESET_SCN_TIME
	THREAD_ID
	THREAD_SQN
	LOW_SCN
	NEXT_SCN
	DICTIONARY_BEGIN
	DICTIONARY_END
	INFO
	STATUS
V_$LOGMNR_PARAMETERS	END_SCN
	INFO
	STATUS
	START_DATE
	END_DATE

Table 3-3   List of Underlying Tables in Dynamic Views *(continued)*

View	Columns
V_$LOGMNR_PARAMETERS (cont.)	START_SCN
V_$LOGMNR_PROCESS	PID
	SPID
	ROLE
	USERNAME
	SERIAL#
	LATCHWAIT
	LATCHSPIN
V_$LOGMNR_REGION	MEMSTATE
	STATE
	OWNING_PROCESS
V_$LOGMNR_SESSION	SESSION_ID
	SESSION_NAME
	SESSION_STATE
	START_SCNWRP
	START_SCNBAS
	END_SCNWRP
	END_SCNBAS
	SPILL_SCNWRP
	SPILL_SCNBAS

Table 3-3 List of Underlying Tables in Dynamic Views (continued)

View	Columns
V_$LOGMNR_SESSION (cont.)	REQUIRED_SLAVE_NUM
	EAGER_THRESHOLD
	STOPMINING_THRESHOLD
	MEMORY_SIZE
	CLIENT_ID
	DB_ID
	RESET_SCNWRP
	RESET_SCNBAS
	CALLBACK_COUNT
	SLAVE_COUNT
V_$LOGMNR_STATS	SESSION_ID
	NAME
	VALUE
V_$LOGMNR_TRANSACTION	XIDUSN
	XIDSLT
	XIDSQN
	COMMIT_SCNWRP
	COMMIT_SCNBAS
	NUM_CHANGE_RECORD
	FLAGS

Table 3-3 List of Underlying Tables in Dynamic Views (continued)

View	Columns
V_$LOGMNR_TRANSACTION (cont.)	CHUNK_INDEX
	TOTAL_CHUNKS
V_$LOGSTDBY	SERIAL#
	LOGSTDBY_ID
	PID
	TYPE
	STATUS_CODE
	STATUS
	HIGH_SCN
V_$LOGSTDBY_STATS	NAME
	VALUE
V_$LOG_HISTORY	RECID
	STAMP
	THREAD#
	SEQUENCE#
	FIRST_CHANGE#
	FIRST_TIME
	NEXT_CHANGE#
V_$MANAGED_STANDBY	PROCESS
	PID

Table 3-3   List of Underlying Tables in Dynamic Views (continued)

View	Columns
V_$MANAGED_STANDBY (cont.)	STATUS
	CLIENT_PROCESS
	CLIENT_PID
	CLIENT_DBID
	GROUP#
	THREAD#
	SEQUENCE#
	BLOCK#
	BLOCKS
	DELAY_MINS
	KNOWN_AGENTS
	ACTIVE_AGENTS
V_$MAP_COMP_LIST	ELEM_IDX
	NUM_COMP
	COMP1_NAME
	COMP1_VAL
	COMP2_NAME
	COMP2_VAL
	COMP3_NAME
	COMP3_VAL

Table 3-3   List of Underlying Tables in Dynamic Views (continued)

View	Columns
V_$MAP_COMP_LIST (cont.)	COMP4_NAME
	COMP4_VAL
	COMP5_NAME
	COMP5_VAL
V_$MAP_ELEMENT	ELEM_NAME
	ELEM_IDX
	ELEM_CFGID
	ELEM_TYPE
	ELEM_SIZE
	ELEM_NSUBELEM
	ELEM_DESCR
	STRIPE_SIZE
	LIB_IDX
V_$MAP_EXT_ELEMENT	ELEM_IDX
	NUM_ATTRB
	ATTRB1_NAME
	ATTRB1_VAL
	ATTRB2_NAME
	ATTRB2_VAL
	ATTRB3_NAME

Table 3-3 List of Underlying Tables in Dynamic Views (continued)

View	Columns
V_$MAP_EXT_ELEMENT (cont.)	ATTRB3_VAL
	ATTRB4_NAME
	ATTRB4_VAL
	ATTRB5_NAME
	ATTRB5_VAL
V_$MAP_FILE	FILE_MAP_IDX
	FILE_CFGID
	FILE_STATUS
	FILE_NAME
	FILE_TYPE
	FILE_STRUCTURE
	FILE_SIZE
	FILE_NEXTS
	LIB_IDX
V_$MAP_FILE_EXTENT	FILE_MAP_IDX
	EXT_NUM
	EXT_ELEM_OFF
	EXT_SIZE
	EXT_FILE_OFF
	EXT_TYPE

Table 3-3 List of Underlying Tables in Dynamic Views (continued)

View	Columns
V_$MAP_FILE_EXTENT (cont.)	ELEM_IDX
V_$MAP_FILE_IO_STACK	FILE_MAP_IDX
	DEPTH
	ELEM_IDX
	CU_SIZE
	STRIDE
	NUM_CU
	ELEM_OFFSET
	FILE_OFFSET
	DATA_TYPE
	PARITY_POS
	PARITY_PERIOD
	ID
	PARENT_ID
V_$MAP_LIBRARY	LIB_IDX
	LIB_NAME
	VENDOR_NAME
	PROTOCOL_NUM
	VERSION_NUM
	PATH_NAME

Table 3-3 List of Underlying Tables in Dynamic Views *(continued)*

View	Columns
V_$MAP_LIBRARY (cont.)	MAP_FILE
	FILE_CFGID
	MAP_ELEM
	ELEM_CFGID
	MAP_SYNC
V_$MAP_SUBELEMENT	CHILD_IDX
	PARENT_IDX
	SUB_NUM
	SUB_SIZE
	ELEM_OFFSET
	SUB_FLAGS
V_$MAX_ACTIVE_SESS_TARGET_MTH	NAME
V_$MLS_PARAMETERS	NUM
	NAME
	TYPE
	VALUE
	ISDEFAULT
	ISSES_MODIFIABLE
	ISSYS_MODIFIABLE
	ISMODIFIED

Table 3-3 List of Underlying Tables in Dynamic Views (continued)

View	Columns
V_$MLS_PARAMETERS (cont.)	ISADJUSTED
	DESCRIPTION
	UPDATE_COMMENT
V_$MTS	MAXIMUM_CONNECTIONS
	MAXIMUM_SESSIONS
	SERVERS_STARTED
	SERVERS_TERMINATED
	SERVERS_HIGHWATER
V_$MTTR_TARGET_ADVICE	MTTR_TARGET_FOR_ESTIMATE
	ADVICE_STATUS
	DIRTY_LIMIT
	ESTD_CACHE_WRITES
	ESTD_CACHE_WRITE_FACTOR
	ESTD_TOTAL_WRITES
	ESTD_TOTAL_WRITE_FACTOR
	ESTD_TOTAL_IOS
	ESTD_TOTAL_IO_FACTOR
V_$MVREFRESH	SID
	SERIAL#
	CURRMVOWNER

Table 3-3   List of Underlying Tables in Dynamic Views (continued)

View	Columns
V_$MVREFRESH (cont.)	CURRMVNAME
V_$MYSTAT	SID
	STATISTIC#
	VALUE
V_$NLS_PARAMETERS	PARAMETER
	VALUE
V_$NLS_VALID_VALUES	PARAMETER
	VALUE
V_$OBJECT_DEPENDENCY	FROM_ADDRESS
	FROM_HASH
	TO_OWNER
	TO_NAME
	TO_ADDRESS
	TO_HASH
	TO_TYPE
V_$OBSOLETE_PARAMETER	NAME
	ISSPECIFIED
V_$OFFLINE_RANGE	RECID
	STAMP
	FILE#

Table 3-3   List of Underlying Tables in Dynamic Views (continued)

View	Columns
V_$OFFLINE_RANGE (cont.)	OFFLINE_CHANGE#
	ONLINE_CHANGE#
	ONLINE_TIME
V_$OPEN_CURSOR	SADDR
	SID
	USER_NAME
	ADDRESS
	HASH_VALUE
	SQL_TEXT
V_$OPTION	PARAMETER
	VALUE
V_$PARALLEL_DEGREE_LIMIT_MTH	NAME
V_$PARAMETER	NUM
	NAME
	TYPE
	VALUE
	ISDEFAULT
	ISSES_MODIFIABLE
	ISSYS_MODIFIABLE
	ISMODIFIED

Table 3-3 List of Underlying Tables in Dynamic Views (continued)

View	Columns
V_$PARAMETER (cont.)	ISADJUSTED
	DESCRIPTION
	UPDATE_COMMENT
V_$PARAMETER2	NUM
	NAME
	TYPE
	VALUE
	ISDEFAULT
	ISSES_MODIFIABLE
	ISSYS_MODIFIABLE
	ISMODIFIED
	ISADJUSTED
	DESCRIPTION
	ORDINAL
	UPDATE_COMMENT
V_$PGASTAT	NAME
	VALUE
	UNIT
V_$PGA_TARGET_ADVICE	PGA_TARGET_FOR_ESTIMATE
	PGA_TARGET_FACTOR

Table 3-3   List of Underlying Tables in Dynamic Views (continued)

View	Columns
V_$PGA_TARGET_ADVICE (cont.)	ADVICE_STATUS
	BYTES_PROCESSED
	ESTD_EXTRA_BYTES_RW
	ESTD_PGA_CACHE_HIT_PERCENTAGE
	ESTD_OVERALLOC_COUNT
V_$PGA_TARGET_ADVICE_HISTOGRAM	PGA_TARGET_FOR_ESTIMATE
	PGA_TARGET_FACTOR
	ADVICE_STATUS
	LOW_OPTIMAL_SIZE
	HIGH_OPTIMAL_SIZE
	ESTD_OPTIMAL_EXECUTIONS
	ESTD_ONEPASS_EXECUTIONS
	ESTD_MULTIPASSES_EXECUTIONS
	ESTD_TOTAL_EXECUTIONS
	IGNORED_WORKAREAS_COUNT
V_$PQ_SESSTAT	STATISTIC
	LAST_QUERY
	SESSION_TOTAL
V_$PQ_SLAVE	SLAVE_NAME
	STATUS

Table 3-3 List of Underlying Tables in Dynamic Views (continued)

View	Columns
V_$PQ_SLAVE (cont.)	SESSIONS
	IDLE_TIME_CUR
	BUSY_TIME_CUR
	CPU_SECS_CUR
	MSGS_SENT_CUR
	MSGS_RCVD_CUR
	IDLE_TIME_TOTAL
	BUSY_TIME_TOTAL
	CPU_SECS_TOTAL
	MSGS_SENT_TOTAL
	MSGS_RCVD_TOTAL
V_$PQ_SYSSTAT	STATISTIC
	VALUE
V_$PQ_TQSTAT	DFO_NUMBER
	TQ_ID
	SERVER_TYPE
	NUM_ROWS
	BYTES
	OPEN_TIME
	AVG_LATENCY

Table 3-3   List of Underlying Tables in Dynamic Views (continued)

View	Columns
V_$PQ_TQSTAT (cont.)	WAITS
	TIMEOUTS
	PROCESS
	INSTANCE
V_$PROCESS	ADDR
	PID
	SPID
	USERNAME
	SERIAL#
	TERMINAL
	PROGRAM
	TRACEID
	BACKGROUND
	LATCHWAIT
	LATCHSPIN
	PGA_USED_MEM
	PGA_ALLOC_MEM
	PGA_FREEABLE_MEM
	PGA_MAX_MEM
V_$PROXY_ARCHIVEDLOG	RECID

Table 3-3 List of Underlying Tables in Dynamic Views (continued)

View	Columns
V_$PROXY_ARCHIVEDLOG (cont.)	STAMP
	DEVICE_TYPE
	HANDLE
	COMMENTS
	MEDIA
	MEDIA_POOL
	STATUS
	DELETED
	THREAD#
	SEQUENCE#
	RESETLOGS_CHANGE#
	RESETLOGS_TIME
	FIRST_CHANGE#
	FIRST_TIME
	NEXT_CHANGE#
	NEXT_TIME
	BLOCKS
	BLOCK_SIZE
	START_TIME
	COMPLETION_TIME

Table 3-3   List of Underlying Tables in Dynamic Views (continued)

View	Columns
V_$PROXY_ARCHIVEDLOG (cont.)	ELAPSED_SECONDS
V_$PROXY_DATAFILE	RECID
	STAMP
	DEVICE_TYPE
	HANDLE
	COMMENTS
	MEDIA
	MEDIA_POOL
	TAG
	STATUS
	DELETED
	FILE#
	CREATION_CHANGE#
	CREATION_TIME
	RESETLOGS_CHANGE#
	RESETLOGS_TIME
	CHECKPOINT_CHANGE#
	CHECKPOINT_TIME
	ABSOLUTE_FUZZY_CHANGE#
	RECOVERY_FUZZY_CHANGE#

Table 3-3 List of Underlying Tables in Dynamic Views (continued)

View	Columns
V_$PROXY_DATAFILE (cont.)	RECOVERY_FUZZY_TIME
	INCREMENTAL_LEVEL
	ONLINE_FUZZY
	BACKUP_FUZZY
	BLOCKS
	BLOCK_SIZE
	OLDEST_OFFLINE_RANGE
	START_TIME
	COMPLETION_TIME
	ELAPSED_SECONDS
	CONTROLFILE_TYPE
	KEEP
	KEEP_UNTIL
	KEEP_OPTIONS
V_$PWFILE_USERS	USERNAME
	SYSDBA
	SYSOPER
V_$PX_PROCESS	SERVER_NAME
	STATUS
	PID

Table 3-3 List of Underlying Tables in Dynamic Views (continued)

View	Columns
V_$PX_PROCESS (cont.)	SPID
	SID
	SERIAL#
V_$PX_PROCESS_SYSSTAT	STATISTIC
	VALUE
V_$PX_SESSION	SADDR
	SID
	SERIAL#
	QCSID
	QCSERIAL#
	QCINST_ID
	SERVER_GROUP
	SERVER_SET
	SERVER#
	DEGREE
	REQ_DEGREE
V_$PX_SESSTAT	SADDR
	SID
	SERIAL#
	QCSID

Table 3-3 List of Underlying Tables in Dynamic Views (continued)

View	Columns
V_$PX_SESSTAT (cont.)	QCSERIAL#
	QCINST_ID
	SERVER_GROUP
	SERVER_SET
	SERVER#
	DEGREE
	REQ_DEGREE
	STATISTIC#
	VALUE
V_$QUEUE	PADDR
	TYPE
	QUEUED
	WAIT
	TOTALQ
V_$QUEUEING_MTH	NAME
V_$RECOVERY_FILE_STATUS	FILENUM
	FILENAME
	STATUS
V_$RECOVERY_LOG	THREAD#
	SEQUENCE#

Table 3-3 List of Underlying Tables in Dynamic Views (continued)

View	Columns
V_$RECOVERY_LOG (cont.)	TIME
	ARCHIVE_NAME
V_$RECOVERY_PROGRESS	TYPE
	ITEM
	SOFAR
	TOTAL
V_$RECOVERY_STATUS	RECOVERY_CHECKPOINT
	THREAD
	SEQUENCE_NEEDED
	SCN_NEEDED
	TIME_NEEDED
	PREVIOUS_LOG_NAME
	PREVIOUS_LOG_STATUS
	REASON
V_$RECOVER_FILE	FILE#
	ONLINE
	ONLINE_STATUS
	ERROR
	CHANGE#
	TIME

Table 3-3   List of Underlying Tables in Dynamic Views (continued)

View	Columns
V_$REPLPROP	SID
	SERIAL#
	NAME
	DBLINK
	STATE
	XID
	SEQUENCE
V_$REPLQUEUE	TXNS_ENQUEUED
	CALLS_ENQUEUED
	TXNS_PURGED
	LAST_ENQUEUE_TIME
	LAST_PURGE_TIME
V_$REQDIST	BUCKET
	COUNT
V_$RESERVED_WORDS	KEYWORD
	LENGTH
V_$RESOURCE	ADDR
	TYPE
	ID1
	ID2

Table 3-3   List of Underlying Tables in Dynamic Views (continued)

View	Columns
V_$RESOURCE_LIMIT	RESOURCE_NAME
	CURRENT_UTILIZATION
	MAX_UTILIZATION
	INITIAL_ALLOCATION
	LIMIT_VALUE
V_$RESUMABLE	ADDR
	SID
	ENABLED
	STATUS
	TIMEOUT
	SUSPEND_TIME
	RESUME_TIME
	NAME
	ERROR_NUMBER
	ERROR_PARAMETER1
	ERROR_PARAMETER2
	ERROR_PARAMETER3
	ERROR_PARAMETER4
	ERROR_PARAMETER5
	ERROR_MSG

Table 3-3   List of Underlying Tables in Dynamic Views (continued)

View	Columns
V_$RMAN_CONFIGURATION	CONF#
	NAME
	VALUE
V_$ROLLNAME	USN
	NAME
V_$ROLLSTAT	USN
	LATCH
	EXTENTS
	RSSIZE
	WRITES
	XACTS
	GETS
	WAITS
	OPTSIZE
	HWMSIZE
	SHRINKS
	WRAPS
	EXTENDS
	AVESHRINK
	AVEACTIVE

Table 3-3 List of Underlying Tables in Dynamic Views (continued)

View	Columns
V_$ROLLSTAT (cont.)	STATUS
	CUREXT
	CURBLK
V_$ROWCACHE	CACHE#
	TYPE
	SUBORDINATE#
	PARAMETER
	COUNT
	USAGE
	FIXED
	GETS
	GETMISSES
	SCANS
	SCANMISSES
	SCANCOMPLETES
	MODIFICATIONS
	FLUSHES
	DLM_REQUESTS
	DLM_CONFLICTS
	DLM_RELEASES

Table 3-3 List of Underlying Tables in Dynamic Views (continued)

View	Columns
V_$ROWCACHE_PARENT	INDX
	HASH
	ADDRESS
	CACHE#
	CACHE_NAME
	EXISTENT
	LOCK_MODE
	LOCK_REQUEST
	TXN
	SADDR
	INST_LOCK_REQUEST
	INST_LOCK_RELEASE
	INST_LOCK_TYPE
	INST_LOCK_ID1
	INST_LOCK_ID2
	KEY
V_$ROWCACHE_SUBORDINATE	INDX
	HASH
	ADDRESS
	CACHE#

Table 3-3 List of Underlying Tables in Dynamic Views (continued)

View	Columns
V_$ROWCACHE_SUBORDINATE (cont.)	SUBCACHE#
	SUBCACHE_NAME
	EXISTENT
	PARENT
	KEY
V_$RSRC_CONSUMER_GROUP	NAME
	ACTIVE_SESSIONS
	EXECUTION_WAITERS
	REQUESTS
	CPU_WAIT_TIME
	CPU_WAITS
	CONSUMED_CPU_TIME
	YIELDS
	QUEUE_LENGTH
	CURRENT_UNDO_CONSUMPTION
V_$RSRC_CONSUMER_GROUP_CPU_MTH	NAME
V_$RSRC_PLAN	NAME
V_$RSRC_PLAN_CPU_MTH	NAME
V_$SEGMENT_STATISTICS	OWNER
	OBJECT_NAME

Table 3-3 List of Underlying Tables in Dynamic Views (continued)

View	Columns
V_$SEGMENT_STATISTICS (cont.)	SUBOBJECT_NAME
	TABLESPACE_NAME
	TS#
	OBJ#
	DATAOBJ#
	OBJECT_TYPE
	STATISTIC_NAME
	STATISTIC#
	VALUE
V_$SEGSTAT	TS#
	OBJ#
	DATAOBJ#
	STATISTIC_NAME
	STATISTIC#
	VALUE
V_$SEGSTAT_NAME	STATISTIC#
	NAME
	SAMPLED
V_$SESSION	SADDR
	SID

Table 3-3   List of Underlying Tables in Dynamic Views (continued)

View	Columns
V_$SESSION (cont.)	SERIAL#
	AUDSID
	PADDR
	USER#
	USERNAME
	COMMAND
	OWNERID
	TADDR
	LOCKWAIT
	STATUS
	SERVER
	SCHEMA#
	SCHEMANAME
	OSUSER
	PROCESS
	MACHINE
	TERMINAL
	PROGRAM
	TYPE
	SQL_ADDRESS

Table 3-3 List of Underlying Tables in Dynamic Views (continued)

View	Columns
V_$SESSION (cont.)	SQL_HASH_VALUE
	PREV_SQL_ADDR
	PREV_HASH_VALUE
	MODULE
	MODULE_HASH
	ACTION
	ACTION_HASH
	CLIENT_INFO
	FIXED_TABLE_SEQUENCE
	ROW_WAIT_OBJ#
	ROW_WAIT_FILE#
	ROW_WAIT_BLOCK#
	ROW_WAIT_ROW#
	LOGON_TIME
	LAST_CALL_ET
	PDML_ENABLED
	FAILOVER_TYPE
	FAILOVER_METHOD
	FAILED_OVER
	RESOURCE_CONSUMER_GROUP

Table 3-3   List of Underlying Tables in Dynamic Views (continued)

View	Columns
V_$SESSION (cont.)	PDML_STATUS
	PDDL_STATUS
	PQ_STATUS
	CURRENT_QUEUE_DURATION
	CLIENT_IDENTIFIER
V_$SESSION_CONNECT_INFO	SID
	AUTHENTICATION_TYPE
	OSUSER
	NETWORK_SERVICE_BANNER
V_$SESSION_CURSOR_CACHE	MAXIMUM
	COUNT
	OPENED_ONCE
	OPEN
	OPENS
	HITS
	HIT_RATIO
V_$SESSION_EVENT	SID
	EVENT
	TOTAL_WAITS
	TOTAL_TIMEOUTS

Table 3-3 List of Underlying Tables in Dynamic Views (continued)

View	Columns
V_$SESSION_EVENT (cont.)	TIME_WAITED
	AVERAGE_WAIT
	MAX_WAIT
	TIME_WAITED_MICRO
V_$SESSION_LONGOPS	SID
	SERIAL#
	OPNAME
	TARGET
	TARGET_DESC
	SOFAR
	TOTALWORK
	UNITS
	START_TIME
	LAST_UPDATE_TIME
	TIME_REMAINING
	ELAPSED_SECONDS
	CONTEXT
	MESSAGE
	USERNAME
	SQL_ADDRESS

Table 3-3   List of Underlying Tables in Dynamic Views (continued)

View	Columns
V_$SESSION_LONGOPS (cont.)	SQL_HASH_VALUE
	QCSID
V_$SESSION_OBJECT_CACHE	PINS
	HITS
	TRUE_HITS
	HIT_RATIO
	TRUE_HIT_RATIO
	OBJECT_REFRESHES
	CACHE_REFRESHES
	OBJECT_FLUSHES
	CACHE_FLUSHES
	CACHE_SHRINKS
	CACHED_OBJECTS
	PINNED_OBJECTS
	CACHE_SIZE
	OPTIMAL_SIZE
	MAXIMUM_SIZE
V_$SESSION_WAIT	SID
	SEQ#
	EVENT

Table 3-3 List of Underlying Tables in Dynamic Views (continued)

View	Columns
V_$SESSION_WAIT (cont.)	P1TEXT
	P1
	P1RAW
	P2TEXT
	P2
	P2RAW
	P3TEXT
	P3
	P3RAW
	WAIT_TIME
	SECONDS_IN_WAIT
	STATE
V_$SESSTAT	SID
	STATISTIC#
	VALUE
V_$SESS_IO	SID
	BLOCK_GETS
	CONSISTENT_GETS
	PHYSICAL_READS
	BLOCK_CHANGES

Table 3-3   List of Underlying Tables in Dynamic Views (continued)

View	Columns
V_$SESS_IO (cont.)	CONSISTENT_CHANGES
V_$SGA	NAME
	VALUE
V_$SGASTAT	POOL
	NAME
	BYTES
V_$SGA_CURRENT_RESIZE_OPS	COMPONENT
	OPER_TYPE
	OPER_MODE
	PARAMETER
	INITIAL_SIZE
	TARGET_SIZE
	CURRENT_SIZE
	START_TIME
	LAST_UPDATE_TIME
V_$SGA_DYNAMIC_COMPONENTS	COMPONENT
	CURRENT_SIZE
	MIN_SIZE
	MAX_SIZE
	OPER_COUNT

Table 3-3 List of Underlying Tables in Dynamic Views (continued)

View	Columns
V_$SGA_DYNAMIC_COMPONENTS (cont.)	LAST_OPER_TYPE
	LAST_OPER_MODE
	LAST_OPER_TIME
	GRANULE_SIZE
V_$SGA_DYNAMIC_FREE_MEMORY	CURRENT_SIZE
V_$SGA_RESIZE_OPS	COMPONENT
	OPER_TYPE
	OPER_MODE
	PARAMETER
	INITIAL_SIZE
	TARGET_SIZE
	FINAL_SIZE
	STATUS
	START_TIME
	END_TIME
V_$SHARED_POOL_ADVICE	SHARED_POOL_SIZE_FOR_ESTIMATE
	SHARED_POOL_SIZE_FACTOR
	ESTD_LC_SIZE
	ESTD_LC_MEMORY_OBJECTS
	ESTD_LC_TIME_SAVED

Table 3-3   List of Underlying Tables in Dynamic Views (continued)

View	Columns
V_$SHARED_POOL_ADVICE (cont.)	ESTD_LC_TIME_SAVED_FACTOR
	ESTD_LC_MEMORY_OBJECT_HITS
V_$SHARED_POOL_RESERVED	FREE_SPACE
	AVG_FREE_SIZE
	FREE_COUNT
	MAX_FREE_SIZE
	USED_SPACE
	AVG_USED_SIZE
	USED_COUNT
	MAX_USED_SIZE
	REQUESTS
	REQUEST_MISSES
	LAST_MISS_SIZE
	MAX_MISS_SIZE
	REQUEST_FAILURES
	LAST_FAILURE_SIZE
	ABORTED_REQUEST_THRESHOLD
	ABORTED_REQUESTS
	LAST_ABORTED_SIZE
V_$SHARED_SERVER	NAME

Table 3-3 List of Underlying Tables in Dynamic Views (continued)

View	Columns
V_$SHARED_SERVER (cont.)	PADDR
	STATUS
	MESSAGES
	BYTES
	BREAKS
	CIRCUIT
	IDLE
	BUSY
	REQUESTS
V_$SHARED_SERVER_MONITOR	MAXIMUM_CONNECTIONS
	MAXIMUM_SESSIONS
	SERVERS_STARTED
	SERVERS_TERMINATED
	SERVERS_HIGHWATER
V_$SORT_SEGMENT	TABLESPACE_NAME
	SEGMENT_FILE
	SEGMENT_BLOCK
	EXTENT_SIZE
	CURRENT_USERS
	TOTAL_EXTENTS

Table 3-3   List of Underlying Tables in Dynamic Views (continued)

View	Columns
V_$SORT_SEGMENT (cont.)	TOTAL_BLOCKS
	USED_EXTENTS
	USED_BLOCKS
	FREE_EXTENTS
	FREE_BLOCKS
	ADDED_EXTENTS
	EXTENT_HITS
	FREED_EXTENTS
	FREE_REQUESTS
	MAX_SIZE
	MAX_BLOCKS
	MAX_USED_SIZE
	MAX_USED_BLOCKS
	MAX_SORT_SIZE
	MAX_SORT_BLOCKS
	RELATIVE_FNO
V_$TEMPSEG_USAGE	USERNAME
V_$SORT_USAGE	USERNAME
V_$TEMPSEG_USAGE	USER
V_$SORT_USAGE	USER

Table 3-3   List of Underlying Tables in Dynamic Views (continued)

View	Columns
V_$TEMPSEG_USAGE	SESSION_ADDR
V_$SORT_USAGE	SESSION_ADDR
V_$TEMPSEG_USAGE	SESSION_NUM
V_$SORT_USAGE	SESSION_NUM
V_$TEMPSEG_USAGE	SQLADDR
V_$SORT_USAGE	SQLADDR
V_$TEMPSEG_USAGE	SQLHASH
V_$SORT_USAGE	SQLHASH
V_$TEMPSEG_USAGE	TABLESPACE
V_$SORT_USAGE	TABLESPACE
V_$TEMPSEG_USAGE	CONTENTS
V_$SORT_USAGE	CONTENTS
V_$TEMPSEG_USAGE	SEGTYPE
V_$SORT_USAGE	SEGTYPE
V_$TEMPSEG_USAGE	SEGFILE#
V_$SORT_USAGE	SEGFILE#
V_$TEMPSEG_USAGE	SEGBLK#
V_$SORT_USAGE	SEGBLK#
V_$TEMPSEG_USAGE	EXTENTS
V_$SORT_USAGE	EXTENTS

Table 3-3   List of Underlying Tables in Dynamic Views (continued)

View	Columns
V_$TEMPSEG_USAGE	BLOCKS
V_$SORT_USAGE	BLOCKS
V_$TEMPSEG_USAGE	SEGRFNO#
V_$SORT_USAGE	SEGRFNO#
V_$SPPARAMETER	SID
	NAME
	VALUE
	ISSPECIFIED
	ORDINAL
	UPDATE_COMMENT
V_$SQL	IS_OBSOLETE
	CHILD_LATCH
	SQL_TEXT
	SHARABLE_MEM
	PERSISTENT_MEM
	RUNTIME_MEM
	SORTS
	LOADED_VERSIONS
	OPEN_VERSIONS
	USERS_OPENING

Table 3-3 List of Underlying Tables in Dynamic Views (continued)

View	Columns
V_$SQL (cont.)	FETCHES
	EXECUTIONS
	USERS_EXECUTING
	LOADS
	FIRST_LOAD_TIME
	INVALIDATIONS
	PARSE_CALLS
	DISK_READS
	BUFFER_GETS
	ROWS_PROCESSED
	COMMAND_TYPE
	OPTIMIZER_MODE
	OPTIMIZER_COST
	PARSING_USER_ID
	PARSING_SCHEMA_ID
	KEPT_VERSIONS
	ADDRESS
	TYPE_CHK_HEAP
	HASH_VALUE
	PLAN_HASH_VALUE

Table 3-3 List of Underlying Tables in Dynamic Views (continued)

View	Columns
V_$SQL (cont.)	CHILD_NUMBER
	MODULE
	MODULE_HASH
	ACTION
	ACTION_HASH
	SERIALIZABLE_ABORTS
	OUTLINE_CATEGORY
	CPU_TIME
	ELAPSED_TIME
	OUTLINE_SID
	CHILD_ADDRESS
	SQLTYPE
	REMOTE
	OBJECT_STATUS
	LITERAL_HASH_VALUE
	LAST_LOAD_TIME
V_$SQLAREA	SQL_TEXT
	SHARABLE_MEM
	PERSISTENT_MEM
	RUNTIME_MEM

Table 3-3 List of Underlying Tables in Dynamic Views (continued)

View	Columns
V_$SQLAREA (cont.)	SORTS
	VERSION_COUNT
	LOADED_VERSIONS
	OPEN_VERSIONS
	USERS_OPENING
	FETCHES
	EXECUTIONS
	USERS_EXECUTING
	LOADS
	FIRST_LOAD_TIME
	INVALIDATIONS
	PARSE_CALLS
	DISK_READS
	BUFFER_GETS
	ROWS_PROCESSED
	COMMAND_TYPE
	OPTIMIZER_MODE
	PARSING_USER_ID
	PARSING_SCHEMA_ID
	KEPT_VERSIONS

Table 3-3   List of Underlying Tables in Dynamic Views (continued)

View	Columns
V_$SQLAREA (cont.)	ADDRESS
	HASH_VALUE
	MODULE
	MODULE_HASH
	ACTION
	ACTION_HASH
	SERIALIZABLE_ABORTS
	CPU_TIME
	ELAPSED_TIME
	IS_OBSOLETE
	CHILD_LATCH
V_$SQLTEXT	ADDRESS
	HASH_VALUE
	COMMAND_TYPE
	PIECE
	SQL_TEXT
V_$SQLTEXT_WITH_NEWLINES	ADDRESS
	HASH_VALUE
	COMMAND_TYPE
	PIECE

Table 3-3 List of Underlying Tables in Dynamic Views (continued)

View	Columns
V_$SQLTEXT_WITH_NEWLINES (cont.)	SQL_TEXT
V_$SQLXS	SQL_TEXT
	SHARABLE_MEM
	SORTS
	MODULE
	LOADED_VERSIONS
	EXECUTIONS
	LOADS
	INVALIDATIONS
	PARSE_CALLS
	DISK_READS
	BUFFER_GETS
	ROWS_PROCESSED
	ADDRESS
	HASH_VALUE
	VERSION_COUNT
V_$SQL_BIND_DATA	CURSOR_NUM
	POSITION
	DATATYPE
	SHARED_MAX_LEN

Table 3-3 List of Underlying Tables in Dynamic Views (continued)

View	Columns
V_$SQL_BIND_DATA (cont.)	PRIVATE_MAX_LEN
	ARRAY_SIZE
	PRECISION
	SCALE
	SHARED_FLAG
	SHARED_FLAG2
	BUF_ADDRESS
	BUF_LENGTH
	VAL_LENGTH
	BUF_FLAG
	INDICATOR
	VALUE
V_$SQL_BIND_METADATA	ADDRESS
	POSITION
	DATATYPE
	MAX_LENGTH
	ARRAY_LEN
	BIND_NAME
V_$SQL_CURSOR	CURNO
	FLAG

Table 3-3 List of Underlying Tables in Dynamic Views (continued)

View	Columns
V_$SQL_CURSOR (cont.)	STATUS
	PARENT_HANDLE
	PARENT_LOCK
	CHILD_LOCK
	CHILD_PIN
	PERS_HEAP_MEM
	WORK_HEAP_MEM
	BIND_VARS
	DEFINE_VARS
	BIND_MEM_LOC
	INST_FLAG
	INST_FLAG2
V_$SQL_PLAN	ADDRESS
	HASH_VALUE
	CHILD_NUMBER
	OPERATION
	OPTIONS
	OBJECT_NODE
	OBJECT#
	OBJECT_OWNER

Table 3-3 List of Underlying Tables in Dynamic Views (continued)

View	Columns
V_$SQL_PLAN (cont.)	OBJECT_NAME
	OPTIMIZER
	ID
	PARENT_ID
	DEPTH
	POSITION
	SEARCH_COLUMNS
	COST
	CARDINALITY
	BYTES
	OTHER_TAG
	PARTITION_START
	PARTITION_STOP
	PARTITION_ID
	OTHER
	DISTRIBUTION
	CPU_COST
	IO_COST
	TEMP_SPACE
	ACCESS_PREDICATES

Table 3-3 List of Underlying Tables in Dynamic Views (continued)

View	Columns
V_$SQL_PLAN (cont.)	FILTER_PREDICATES
V_$SQL_PLAN_STATISTICS	ADDRESS
	HASH_VALUE
	CHILD_NUMBER
	OPERATION_ID
	EXECUTIONS
	LAST_STARTS
	STARTS
	LAST_OUTPUT_ROWS
	OUTPUT_ROWS
	LAST_CR_BUFFER_GETS
	CR_BUFFER_GETS
	LAST_CU_BUFFER_GETS
	CU_BUFFER_GETS
	LAST_DISK_READS
	DISK_READS
	LAST_DISK_WRITES
	DISK_WRITES
	LAST_ELAPSED_TIME
	ELAPSED_TIME

Table 3-3   List of Underlying Tables in Dynamic Views (continued)

View	Columns
V_$SQL_PLAN_STATISTICS_ALL	PARENT_ID
	DEPTH
	POSITION
	SEARCH_COLUMNS
	COST
	CARDINALITY
	BYTES
	OTHER_TAG
	PARTITION_START
	PARTITION_STOP
	PARTITION_ID
	OTHER
	DISTRIBUTION
	CPU_COST
	IO_COST
	TEMP_SPACE
	ACCESS_PREDICATES
	FILTER_PREDICATES
	EXECUTIONS
	LAST_STARTS

Table 3-3 List of Underlying Tables in Dynamic Views (continued)

View	Columns
V_$SQL_PLAN_STATISTICS_ALL (cont.)	STARTS
	LAST_OUTPUT_ROWS
	OUTPUT_ROWS
	LAST_CR_BUFFER_GETS
	CR_BUFFER_GETS
	LAST_CU_BUFFER_GETS
	CU_BUFFER_GETS
	LAST_DISK_READS
	DISK_READS
	LAST_DISK_WRITES
	DISK_WRITES
	LAST_ELAPSED_TIME
	ELAPSED_TIME
	POLICY
	ESTIMATED_OPTIMAL_SIZE
	ESTIMATED_ONEPASS_SIZE
	LAST_MEMORY_USED
	LAST_EXECUTION
	LAST_DEGREE
	TOTAL_EXECUTIONS

Table 3-3   List of Underlying Tables in Dynamic Views (continued)

View	Columns
V_$SQL_PLAN_STATISTICS_ALL (cont.)	OPTIMAL_EXECUTIONS
	ONEPASS_EXECUTIONS
	MULTIPASSES_EXECUTIONS
	ACTIVE_TIME
	MAX_TEMPSEG_SIZE
	LAST_TEMPSEG_SIZE
	ADDRESS
	HASH_VALUE
	CHILD_NUMBER
	OPERATION
	OPTIONS
	OBJECT_NODE
	OBJECT#
	OBJECT_OWNER
	OBJECT_NAME
	OPTIMIZER
	ID
V_$SQL_REDIRECTION	ADDRESS
	PARENT_HANDLE
	HASH_VALUE

Table 3-3 List of Underlying Tables in Dynamic Views (continued)

View	Columns
V_$SQL_REDIRECTION (cont.)	CHILD_NUMBER
	PARSING_USER_ID
	PARSING_SCHEMA_ID
	COMMAND_TYPE
	REASON
	ERROR_CODE
	POSITION
	SQL_TEXT_PIECE
	ERROR_MESSAGE
V_$SQL_SHARED_CURSOR	ADDRESS
	KGLHDPAR
	UNBOUND_CURSOR
	SQL_TYPE_MISMATCH
	OPTIMIZER_MISMATCH
	OUTLINE_MISMATCH
	STATS_ROW_MISMATCH
	LITERAL_MISMATCH
	SEC_DEPTH_MISMATCH
	EXPLAIN_PLAN_CURSOR
	BUFFERED_DML_MISMATCH

Table 3-3 List of Underlying Tables in Dynamic Views (continued)

View	Columns
V_$SQL_SHARED_CURSOR (cont.)	PDML_ENV_MISMATCH
	INST_DRTLD_MISMATCH
	SLAVE_QC_MISMATCH
	TYPECHECK_MISMATCH
	AUTH_CHECK_MISMATCH
	BIND_MISMATCH
	DESCRIBE_MISMATCH
	LANGUAGE_MISMATCH
	TRANSLATION_MISMATCH
	ROW_LEVEL_SEC_MISMATCH
	INSUFF_PRIVS
	INSUFF_PRIVS_REM
	REMOTE_TRANS_MISMATCH
	LOGMINER_SESSION_MISMATCH
	INCOMP_LTRL_MISMATCH
	OVERLAP_TIME_MISMATCH
	SQL_REDIRECT_MISMATCH
	MV_QUERY_GEN_MISMATCH
	USER_BIND_PEEK_MISMATCH
	TYPCHK_DEP_MISMATCH

Table 3-3 List of Underlying Tables in Dynamic Views (continued)

View	Columns
V_$SQL_SHARED_CURSOR (cont.)	NO_TRIGGER_MISMATCH
	FLASHBACK_CURSOR
V_$SQL_SHARED_MEMORY	SQL_TEXT
	HASH_VALUE
	HEAP_DESC
	STRUCTURE
	FUNCTION
	CHUNK_COM
	CHUNK_PTR
	CHUNK_SIZE
	ALLOC_CLASS
	CHUNK_TYPE
	SUBHEAP_DESC
V_$SQL_WORKAREA	ADDRESS
	HASH_VALUE
	CHILD_NUMBER
	WORKAREA_ADDRESS
	OPERATION_TYPE
	OPERATION_ID
	POLICY

Table 3-3   List of Underlying Tables in Dynamic Views (continued)

View	Columns
V_$SQL_WORKAREA (cont.)	ESTIMATED_OPTIMAL_SIZE
	ESTIMATED_ONEPASS_SIZE
	LAST_MEMORY_USED
	LAST_EXECUTION
	LAST_DEGREE
	TOTAL_EXECUTIONS
	OPTIMAL_EXECUTIONS
	ONEPASS_EXECUTIONS
	MULTIPASSES_EXECUTIONS
	ACTIVE_TIME
	MAX_TEMPSEG_SIZE
	LAST_TEMPSEG_SIZE
V_$SQL_WORKAREA_ACTIVE	WORKAREA_ADDRESS
	OPERATION_TYPE
	OPERATION_ID
	POLICY
	SID
	QCINST_ID
	QCSID
	ACTIVE_TIME

Table 3-3   List of Underlying Tables in Dynamic Views (continued)

View	Columns
V_$SQL_WORKAREA_ACTIVE (cont.)	WORK_AREA_SIZE
	EXPECTED_SIZE
	ACTUAL_MEM_USED
	MAX_MEM_USED
	NUMBER_PASSES
	TEMPSEG_SIZE
	TABLESPACE
	SEGRFNO#
	SEGBLK#
V_$SQL_WORKAREA_HISTOGRAM	LOW_OPTIMAL_SIZE
	HIGH_OPTIMAL_SIZE
	OPTIMAL_EXECUTIONS
	ONEPASS_EXECUTIONS
	MULTIPASSES_EXECUTIONS
	TOTAL_EXECUTIONS
V_$STANDBY_LOG	GROUP#
	THREAD#
	SEQUENCE#
	BYTES
	USED

Table 3-3 List of Underlying Tables in Dynamic Views (continued)

View	Columns
V_$STANDBY_LOG (cont.)	ARCHIVED
	STATUS
	FIRST_CHANGE#
	FIRST_TIME
	LAST_CHANGE#
	LAST_TIME
V_$STATISTICS_LEVEL	STATISTICS_NAME
	DESCRIPTION
	SESSION_STATUS
	SYSTEM_STATUS
	ACTIVATION_LEVEL
	STATISTICS_VIEW_NAME
	SESSION_SETTABLE
V_$STATNAME	STATISTIC#
	NAME
	CLASS
V_$STREAMS_APPLY_COORDINATOR	SID
	SERIAL#
	STATE
	APPLY#

Table 3-3 List of Underlying Tables in Dynamic Views (continued)

View	Columns
V_$STREAMS_APPLY_COORDINATOR (cont.)	APPLY_NAME
	TOTAL_APPLIED
	TOTAL_WAIT_DEPS
	TOTAL_WAIT_COMMITS
	TOTAL_ADMIN
	TOTAL_ASSIGNED
	TOTAL_RECEIVED
	TOTAL_ERRORS
	LWM_TIME
	LWM_MESSAGE_NUMBER
	LWM_MESSAGE_CREATE_TIME
	HWM_TIME
	HWM_MESSAGE_NUMBER
	HWM_MESSAGE_CREATE_TIME
	STARTUP_TIME
	ELAPSED_SCHEDULE_TIME
V_$STREAMS_APPLY_READER	SID
	SERIAL#
	APPLY#
	APPLY_NAME

Table 3-3   List of Underlying Tables in Dynamic Views (continued)

View	Columns
V_$STREAMS_APPLY_READER (cont.)	STATE
	TOTAL_MESSAGES_DEQUEUED
	DEQUEUE_TIME
	DEQUEUED_MESSAGE_NUMBER
	DEQUEUED_MESSAGE_CREATE_TIME
	SGA_USED
	ELAPSED_DEQUEUE_TIME
	ELAPSED_SCHEDULE_TIME
V_$STREAMS_APPLY_SERVER	SID
	SERIAL#
	APPLY#
	APPLY_NAME
	SERVER_ID
	STATE
	XIDUSN
	XIDSLT
	XIDSQN
	COMMITSCN
	DEP_XIDUSN
	DEP_XIDSLT

Table 3-3 List of Underlying Tables in Dynamic Views (continued)

View	Columns
V_$STREAMS_APPLY_SERVER (cont.)	DEP_XIDSQN
	DEP_COMMITSCN
	MESSAGE_SEQUENCE
	TOTAL_ASSIGNED
	TOTAL_ADMIN
	TOTAL_MESSAGES_APPLIED
	APPLY_TIME
	APPLIED_MESSAGE_NUMBER
	APPLIED_MESSAGE_CREATE_TIME
	ELAPSED_DEQUEUE_TIME
	ELAPSED_APPLY_TIME
V_$STREAMS_CAPTURE	SID
	SERIAL#
	CAPTURE#
	CAPTURE_NAME
	STARTUP_TIME
	STATE
	TOTAL_MESSAGES_CAPTURED
	CAPTURE_TIME
	CAPTURE_MESSAGE_NUMBER

Table 3-3   List of Underlying Tables in Dynamic Views (continued)

View	Columns
V_$STREAMS_CAPTURE (cont.)	CAPTURE_MESSAGE_CREATE_TIME
	TOTAL_MESSAGES_ENQUEUED
	ENQUEUE_TIME
	ENQUEUE_MESSAGE_NUMBER
	ENQUEUE_MESSAGE_CREATE_TIME
	ELAPSED_CAPTURE_TIME
	ELAPSED_RULE_TIME
	ELAPSED_ENQUEUE_TIME
	ELAPSED_LCR_TIME
V_$SUBCACHE	OWNER_NAME
	NAME
	TYPE
	HEAP_NUM
	CACHE_ID
	CACHE_CNT
	HEAP_SZ
	HEAP_ALOC
	HEAP_USED
V_$SYSSTAT	STATISTIC#
	NAME

Table 3-3 List of Underlying Tables in Dynamic Views *(continued)*

View	Columns
V_$SYSSTAT (cont.)	CLASS
	VALUE
V_$SYSTEM_CURSOR_CACHE	OPENS
	HITS
	HIT_RATIO
V_$SYSTEM_EVENT	EVENT
	TOTAL_WAITS
	TOTAL_TIMEOUTS
	TIME_WAITED
	AVERAGE_WAIT
	TIME_WAITED_MICRO
V_$SYSTEM_PARAMETER	NUM
	NAME
	TYPE
	VALUE
	ISDEFAULT
	ISSES_MODIFIABLE
	ISSYS_MODIFIABLE
	ISMODIFIED
	ISADJUSTED

Table 3-3 List of Underlying Tables in Dynamic Views (continued)

View	Columns
V_$SYSTEM_PARAMETER (cont.)	DESCRIPTION
	UPDATE_COMMENT
V_$SYSTEM_PARAMETER2	NUM
	NAME
	TYPE
	VALUE
	ISDEFAULT
	ISSES_MODIFIABLE
	ISSYS_MODIFIABLE
	ISMODIFIED
	ISADJUSTED
	DESCRIPTION
	ORDINAL
	UPDATE_COMMENT
V_$TABLESPACE	TS#
	NAME
	INCLUDED_IN_DATABASE_BACKUP
V_$TEMPFILE	FILE#
	CREATION_CHANGE#
	CREATION_TIME

Table 3-3 List of Underlying Tables in Dynamic Views (continued)

View	Columns
V_$TEMPFILE (cont.)	TS#
	RFILE#
	STATUS
	ENABLED
	BYTES
	BLOCKS
	CREATE_BYTES
	BLOCK_SIZE
	NAME
V_$TEMPORARY_LOBS	SID
	CACHE_LOBS
	NOCACHE_LOBS
V_$TEMPSTAT	FILE#
	PHYRDS
	PHYWRTS
	PHYBLKRD
	PHYBLKWRT
	SINGLEBLKRDS
	READTIM
	WRITETIM

Table 3-3 List of Underlying Tables in Dynamic Views (continued)

View	Columns
V_$TEMPSTAT (cont.)	SINGLEBLKRDTIM
	AVGIOTIM
	LSTIOTIM
	MINIOTIM
	MAXIORTM
	MAXIOWTM
V_$TEMPSTATXS	TSNAME
	FILENAME
	PHYRDS
	PHYWRTS
	READTIM
	WRITETIM
	PHYBLKRD
	PHYBLKWRT
	WAIT_COUNT
	TIME
V_$TEMP_CACHE_TRANSFER	X_2_NULL_FORCED_STALE
	X_2_S
	X_2_S_FORCED_WRITE
	S_2_NULL

Table 3-3 List of Underlying Tables in Dynamic Views (continued)

View	Columns
V_$TEMP_CACHE_TRANSFER (cont.)	S_2_NULL_FORCED_STALE
	RBR
	RBR_FORCED_WRITE
	NULL_2_X
	S_2_X
	NULL_2_S
	FILE_NUMBER
	X_2_NULL
	X_2_NULL_FORCED_WRITE
V_$TEMP_EXTENT_MAP	TABLESPACE_NAME
	FILE_ID
	BLOCK_ID
	BYTES
	BLOCKS
	OWNER
	RELATIVE_FNO
V_$TEMP_EXTENT_POOL	TABLESPACE_NAME
	FILE_ID
	EXTENTS_CACHED
	EXTENTS_USED

Table 3-3   List of Underlying Tables in Dynamic Views (continued)

View	Columns
V_$TEMP_EXTENT_POOL (cont.)	BLOCKS_CACHED
	BLOCKS_USED
	BYTES_CACHED
	BYTES_USED
	RELATIVE_FNO
V_$TEMP_PING	FILE_NUMBER
	FREQUENCY
	X_2_NULL
	X_2_NULL_FORCED_WRITE
	X_2_NULL_FORCED_STALE
	X_2_S
	X_2_S_FORCED_WRITE
	X_2_SSX
	X_2_SSX_FORCED_WRITE
	S_2_NULL
	S_2_NULL_FORCED_STALE
	SS_2_NULL
	SS_2_RLS
	WRB
	WRB_FORCED_WRITE

Table 3-3 List of Underlying Tables in Dynamic Views (continued)

View	Columns
V_$TEMP_PING (cont.)	RBR
	RBR_FORCED_WRITE
	RBR_FORCED_STALE
	CBR
	CBR_FORCED_WRITE
	NULL_2_X
	S_2_X
	SSX_2_X
	NULL_2_S
	NULL_2_SS
	OP_2_SS
V_$TEMP_SPACE_HEADER	TABLESPACE_NAME
	FILE_ID
	BYTES_USED
	BLOCKS_USED
	BYTES_FREE
	BLOCKS_FREE
	RELATIVE_FNO
V_$THREAD	THREAD#
	STATUS

Table 3-3 List of Underlying Tables in Dynamic Views (continued)

View	Columns
V_$THREAD (cont.)	ENABLED
	GROUPS
	INSTANCE
	OPEN_TIME
	CURRENT_GROUP#
	SEQUENCE#
	CHECKPOINT_CHANGE#
	CHECKPOINT_TIME
	ENABLE_CHANGE#
	ENABLE_TIME
	DISABLE_CHANGE#
	DISABLE_TIME
V_$TIMER	HSECS
V_$TIMEZONE_NAMES	TZNAME
	TZABBREV
V_$TRANSACTION	ADDR
	XIDUSN
	XIDSLOT
	XIDSQN
	UBAFIL

Table 3-3 List of Underlying Tables in Dynamic Views (continued)

View	Columns
V_$TRANSACTION (cont.)	UBABLK
	UBASQN
	UBAREC
	STATUS
	START_TIME
	START_SCNB
	START_SCNW
	START_UEXT
	START_UBAFIL
	START_UBABLK
	START_UBASQN
	START_UBAREC
	SES_ADDR
	FLAG
	SPACE
	RECURSIVE
	NOUNDO
	PTX
	NAME
	PRV_XIDUSN

Table 3-3   List of Underlying Tables in Dynamic Views (continued)

View	Columns
V_$TRANSACTION (cont.)	PRV_XIDSLT
	PRV_XIDSQN
	PTX_XIDUSN
	PTX_XIDSLT
	PTX_XIDSQN
	DSCN-B
	DSCN-W
	USED_UBLK
	USED_UREC
	LOG_IO
	PHY_IO
	CR_GET
	CR_CHANGE
V_$TRANSACTION_ENQUEUE	ADDR
	KADDR
	SID
	TYPE
	ID1
	ID2
	LMODE

Table 3-3 List of Underlying Tables in Dynamic Views *(continued)*

View	Columns
V_$TRANSACTION_ENQUEUE (cont.)	REQUEST
	CTIME
	BLOCK
V_$TYPE_SIZE	COMPONENT
	TYPE
	DESCRIPTION
	TYPE_SIZE
V_$UNDOSTAT	BEGIN_TIME
	END_TIME
	UNDOTSN
	UNDOBLKS
	TXNCOUNT
	MAXQUERYLEN
	MAXCONCURRENCY
	UNXPSTEALCNT
	UNXPBLKRELCNT
	UNXPBLKREUCNT
	EXPSTEALCNT
	EXPBLKRELCNT
	EXPBLKREUCNT

Table 3-3 List of Underlying Tables in Dynamic Views (continued)

View	Columns
V_$UNDOSTAT (cont.)	SSOLDERRCNT
	NOSPACEERRCNT
V_$VERSION	BANNER
V_$VPD_POLICY	ADDRESS
	PARADDR
	SQL_HASH
	CHILD_NUMBER
	OBJECT_OWNER
	OBJECT_NAME
	POLICY_GROUP
	POLICY
	POLICY_FUNCTION_OWNER
	PREDICATE
V_$WAITSTAT	CLASS
	COUNT
	TIME
V_$_LOCK	LADDR
	KADDR
	SADDR
	RADDR

Table 3-3   List of Underlying Tables in Dynamic Views (continued)

View	Columns
V_$_LOCK (cont.)	LMODE
	REQUEST
	CTIME
	BLOCK

About Prentice Hall Professional Technical Reference

With origins reaching back to the industry's first computer science publishing program in the 1960s, and formally launched as its own imprint in 1986, Prentice Hall Professional Technical Reference (PH PTR) has developed into the leading provider of technical books in the world today. Our editors now publish over 200 books annually, authored by leaders in the fields of computing, engineering, and business.

Our roots are firmly planted in the soil that gave rise to the technical revolution. Our bookshelf contains many of the industry's computing and engineering classics: Kernighan and Ritchie's *C Programming Language*, Nemeth's *UNIX System Administration Handbook*, Horstmann's *Core Java*, and Johnson's *High-Speed Digital Design*.

PH PTR acknowledges its auspicious beginnings while it looks to the future for inspiration. We continue to evolve and break new ground in publishing by providing today's professionals with tomorrow's solutions.

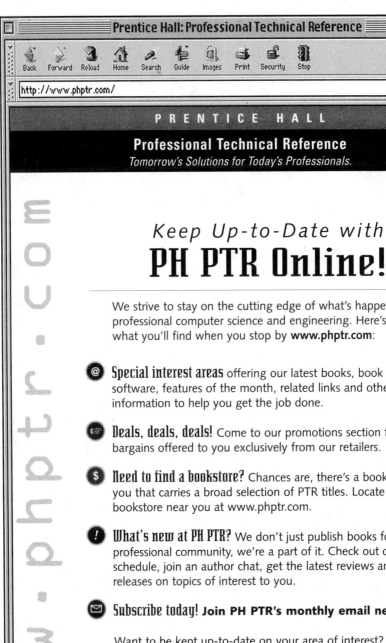